DOCTOR KHUMALO

SOUTH AFRICA

Sikwane Olebile Ntsodi

AuthorHouse™
1663 Liberty Drive
Bloomington, IN 47403
www.authorhouse.com
Phone: 1 (800) 839-8640

Published by AuthorHouse 06/21/2019

ISBN: 978-1-5462-2822-6 (sc)
978-1-5462-2823-3 (e)

Library of Congress Control Number: 2018903834

Print information available on the last page.

Any people depicted in stock imagery provided by Getty Images are models,
and such images are being used for illustrative purposes only.
Certain stock imagery © Getty Images.

This book is printed on acid-free paper.

Because of the dynamic nature of the Internet, any web addresses or links contained in this book may have changed
since publication and may no longer be valid. The views expressed in this work are solely those of the author and do not
necessarily reflect the views of the publisher, and the publisher hereby disclaims any responsibility for them.

authorHOUSE®

DOCTOR KHUMALO

SOUTH AFRICA

Told by Olebile Sikwane

*In the memory of my late grandmother **Mosele Sikwane***

*I wake up every morning because of the values and principles you bequeathed me; that the Lord shall reward people whose life is premised on **love, belief, hard work, empathy, honesty, patience and respect.***

Thank you nkoko.

Sabali!!

CONTENTS

Chapter 1   Meeting Doctor Khumalo 1

Chapter 2   Dube Township, Soweto 5

Chapter 3   The Debut, 1987 11

Chapter 4   Bafana Bafana, 1992 15

Chapter 5   AFCON,1996 31

Chapter 6   France 98, World Cup 58

Chapter 7   Post-France, 1998 75

Chapter 8   The Pretty Boy 78

Chapter 9   16 Valve 82

Chapter 10   The brand, DKSA 88

Chapter 11   Doctor Khumalo (PTY) LTD 94

Chapter 12   Mdokies & The Dawg.. 105

Chapter 13   Argentina 110

Chapter 14   The American Dream 112

Chapter 15   Coaching Kaizer Chiefs 122

Chapter 16   The State v Doctor Khumalo 128

Chapter 17   Life in Retirement 135

Chapter 18   Music & Film 141

What they said

"There has always been debate about who the greatest South African footballer of all time is. This World Cup gives you the opportunity to settle this debate once and for all."-President **Nelson Mandela**,1998

"Whenever people speak about Doctor Khumalo,you can see in their eyes that they mean what they say. He was everything to the people of South Africa."-**Teko Modise**, Bafana Bafana legend

"Footage of the first 45 minutes of that match shows how we made Brazillians look very average,and why i think Doctor Khumalo is the greatest player I have ever worked with."-**Clive Barker**, ex Bafana Bafana Coach

What they said

''Doctor Khumalo was a great player. I watched him play while I was young, and I just wanted to be like him. For his talent, he should have played in Europe.''- **Samuel Eto'o**, ex Barcelona, Chelsea & Inter Milan striker

"Possibly the most celebrated player of his generation and a real poster boy. A true Bafana Bafana legend."-**Walter Mokoena**, Founder; JoburgPost

"Doctor Khumalo is a huge symbol of success to young boys and most of them aspire to be like him. He was by far the most recognizable figure in the Bafana team."-**Neil Tovey**, ex Bafana Bafana captain

''A riveting and deserved account of a modern-day icon of the game. This book captures the story of a player I saw growing up in Dube before he hit the big stage, mesmerizing crowds at school matches. Thank you for documenting the life of a black footballer while he is still alive. Ke nako!''-**Thapelo Moloantoa**, Publisher; Fullcircle, United Kingdom

Prologue

The reader is advised to acknowledge that this story is told conversational style;the African traditional way of telling a story so to speak. This is a fan's perspective. Please tag along in this story. It's a spectacular account of an African township talent who defied Apartheid barriers and reached global stardom-against all odds. The truth is that the story of many African legends is only told when they are no longer alive. That is if that legend is lucky enough to be recognized. In most cases, authorities do it after a public outcry. We all saw this with the iconic Winnie Madikizela-Mandela when she passed on. Julius Malema, Leader of the Economic Freedom Fighters made a public request, aimed at the ANC government, that Cape Town International Airport be renamed after struggle icon Winnie Mandela, bluntly put; ''name it Winnie Madikizela-Mandela International Airport!'' Whether ANC aceeds to that demand is a matter for another day. The truth is that our heroes and heroines never fully get honored in their lifetime especially in Africa. If it's a national hero, politicians often do it for political mileage. This is appalling. I must admit in advance that i admire Doctor Khumalo the player and Doctor Khumalo the brand very much. Everybody and anybody who truly knows me simply knows this fact. I believe that stories of many African greats have not been adequately told in print and in film. Generations behind us need to read, watch and know more about their heroes and heroines. We have a duty to tell these stories now, not tomorrow. Everyday, we read about many European players like Steven Gerrard,Wayne Rooney, Mario Ballitoli, Zlatan Ibrahimovich etc. In the United States, they have long told us the story of Tiger Woods. We know the story of Madonna, Serena Williams and Beyonce now already when they are still alive. The brand Floyd Mayweather has been sold to the world in a manner never seen before. Americans celebrate their own today for tomorrow. Who in the world doesn't know the life story of Kobe Bryant and Michael Jordan? Where United States and Britain have interest, they will sell and market that brand and its story aggressively. American and British corporations are inextricably involved in motor racing. That is why we now know more about Lewis Hamilton. In tennis, it's Serena Williams, Rafael Nadal and Roger Federer(whose mother is an Afrikaaner South African by the way) while Usain Bolt in athletics has been sold to the world in all shapes and forms. We have very little we can say about our own Gelbooi Masango, Thomas Madigage, Tico Tico Bucuane, Scara Thindwa, Tumie Duiker, Ernest Chirwali, Dipsey Selolwane, Ricardo Mannetti, Tresor Mputu and Fabrice Akwa etc. These are African football icons. It is is sad that no one has written the beautiful story of Dr Jomo Sono. Jomo-the golden boy of Orlando Pirates and New York Cosmos. This is blasphemy! I have not seen the story of Abedi Pele or Jay Jay Okocha! I wish to read about the great Kalusha Bwalya of Zambia today, not when he has departed this life. If Africa has not written about Roger Milla, Samuel Eto' and Yaya Toure, then we should be embarrassed as writers. It is hypoctrical of us that we have stocks and piles of books in our living rooms about mega superstars such as Jay Z and Lebron James yet there is no single book on George Weah, the first and only African to win FIFA player of the Year award! George Weah is now State President of Liberia! Doctor Khumalo & Co played a large part of their football during the height of political turmoil that engulfed South Africa. The racist policy got South Africa banned from international soccer. This was catestrophic in many ways. It killed black talent. It literally buried dreams and aspirations of many black people. Doctor Khumalo and his peers did not abandon their dream of becoming global stars.They persevered against all odds. They thrilled and inspired millions of disadvantaged people whose only solace was the smile that football brought to their disenfranchised faces. The beautiful game of football united people in their quest to dismantle Apartheid. Without doubt, football was critically important in collapsing Apartheid. Soccer City became the convergence point in soccer as it was in politics. Nelson Mandela came out of prison to address millions of South Africans and the world. Over 90,000 people packed FNB stadium to see and listen to Mandela on that day. Soccer truly united a deeply divided people. This is the resilience of soccer against oppressive laws of the past where discrimination was deployed to deny blacks an opportunity to study, to play and to even interact with white people. This discrimination impacted both adversely and negatively on the skills of blacks. Black people did not have access to proper facilities to develop their talent not only in sport but also in arts, music, academia etc. This discrimination attracted the penalty of sanctions upon South Africa. This meant that South Africa could not export talent! Doctor Khumalo became a victim of this penalty when several European clubs sought his services in the late 80's and 90's. I am alive to the fact that he had a trial stint with Aston Villa and Crystal Palace and played against Fiorentina of Italy. The prejudice of being a South African black made things difficult for his dream during that time. The story of Doctor Khumalo demonstrates how the power of belief and faith won against arguably the most extraordinarily difficult and convulated political conundrum the world had ever known. This book further demonstrates the role soccer played in re-engineering and transforming the South African political socio-economic landscape into a constitutional dispensation of today. South Africa sports infrastructure is by all accounts, world class today because of South Africa's re-admission into the international community. While I accept that this may not be the full story or the perfect account of things, it is however a subjective story of a journey of my personal hero. It is strictly my view, and in some instances of those who have worked with and against Doctor Khumalo. The fact is that almost every African boy or girl grew up looking upon a hero or heroine of some sort. Doctor Khumalo was and remains my all time sporting hero. Yes ahead of Lionel Messi and Zinedine Zidane. Yes ahead of Mohommed Ali and Usain Bolt. Yes ahead of Mohommed Aboutrika. The reason is simple. You cant regulate love. You just cant explain it. The other fact is that I can relate. I watched Doctor Khumalo during his heyday, live. I have met him. His impact on me is inexplicable. Some people looked up to criminals as their heroes. My hero is not a criminal but a professional footballer who changed and touched many lives in both my two countries and some parts of Africa and the world. I became a writer because of the power and inspiration of Doctor Khumalo in football. Yes, this Doctor Khumalo story may not be a perfectly complete story because of the obvious constraints I encountered to delve into the life of a public figure unauthorized. But this story truly represents an African trajectory of an African child that indeed all our dreams are valid.

Doctor Khumalo was able to dream in the midst of all the gloom of political uncertainty. Indeed, his dream became possible because of the faith and belief he had as an ambitious and committed youngster. The hackneyed narrative that a black child can not succeed because they are from the township is grossly false. The false narrative that legends are honored when they are no longer alive is preposterously dangerous. It has held most of us black people back. I have rejected it through this celebration of my hero. This book is an honor I bestow upon Doctor Khumalo. Now! Ngoku! Kajeko! Today and for tomorrow. I have travelled around the world and seen that anything and everything is possible regardless of one's station in life. The old and hackneyed narrative that life is impossible for black people from disadvantaged backgrounds has generally hamgstrung our thoughts. In the end, we lose endless possibilities presented to us and those already before us. That narrative must fall, ngoku! I chose to write about Doctor Khumalo because he inspired me a great deal as a young boy growing up in Botswana. I grew up in a hopeless Copper-Nickel mining town of Selibe Phikwe, in the east of Botswana. Throughout my boyhood, I believed that I would one day meet Doctor Khumalo. I have. Not once. Not twice. A couple of times. Those who believe in impossibility will never meet Doctor Khumalo. They will never meet their heroes. They will not achieve their dreams. A writer who doesn't believe in his dreams will never write a book. I have always believed that all our dreams are possible if we physically and mentally set out to achieve them. No matter what cynics say or think. Just do it. Now! I saw how Dj Fresh left a very inward-looking Botswana in 1993 for Johannesburg, to pursue his boyhood dream-against all odds-to become what his heart wished for;a top radio Dj. Dj Fresh went beyond that. Today DJ Fresh is a massive brand. He is a multi-millionaire DJ well known around the world, playing with and against the best. Levels!

As a young boy, I was raised in a family which was and still is preoccupied with football. My uncle Shoti Sikwane is Kaizer Chiefs through and through. He is a card carrying Kaizer Chiefs supporter in Botswana! Naturally, as I was growing up, he wanted me to watch all Kaizer Chiefs matches. I would watch their matches religiously on CCV-TV and later on SABC. The player who excited me the most was without doubt Doctor Khumalo. Both my uncle Sikwane and my father played a very important role in my idolizing 16v, as he is fondly known. I remember someday asking my father who between Doctor Khumalo and Ace Ntsoelengoe was the best player. That is long before the Ronaldo/Messi debate that has been ongoing for over a decade now. My father was non-committal. He would never give me an unequivocal answer. I had heard about Ace Ntsoelengoe. I had seen a few clips of him. He seemed to be a smart player, intelligent like Jomo Sono. The reason why my father never really gave me a direct answer was that he obvioulsy preferred Ace Ntsoelengoe more. He had watched Ace Ntsoelengoe many times in Johannesburg. My father had also lived in Randfontein where Ace Ntsoelengoe came from. Ace was a cult figure there. I ingeniously and nippily deduced that he was conflicted. He did not want to 'hurt' me as he had figured out that I was more of a Doctor Khumalo fan than a Kaizer Chiefs fan. For me, Doctor Khumalo then and even now, encapsulates all that which we watch and read about as the beautiful game. He made football look easy. I played soccer at Segomotso Primary. I tried again when I was in Matric at Rosebank House College. I just failed to cut it. My contemporaries at Segomotso Primary notably Mompati Thuma went on to play for the Botswana National Team. I loved Doctor Khumalo so much that even in my game, I had some of his features notably the lack of pace and the penchant for tricks. This is despite my coaches' emphasis on a more direct and quick play. But to be honest, as early as Primary School, after careful consideration, I realized that I would never really cut it at professional football. I swiftly buried that dream after i broke my left hand, two weeks before Primary School Leaving Examinations following a rough tackle from an opponent.

During my gap year in Botswana, before I headed out to embark on Matric in Cape Town-inspired by creative writings of respected soccer writers and experts like the legendary Mark Glesson, Thomas Kwenaite, Richard Maguire, Rodney Reiners, Nelson Rashavha, Trevor Mosehathebe, Sbusiso Mseleku, Ernest Landheer, Neil Creig, Edshine Phosa,Sandile Mchunu, Monwabisi Jimlongo, Andrea Koshiaris, Reginald Nkholise, Bareng-Batho Kortjaas, Jermaine Craig, Clint Roper amongst others, I got a job at a publication called The Mirror as a cub reporter. Here at the age of 19, I reported on sports mostly and Magistrates Court cases. In

2005, i linked up with 365 Digital under Anthony McLennan in Cape Town. McLennan and Thapelo Moloantoa really tutored me. I covered matches, interviewed soccer stars, coaches and club bosses and wrote at a supersonic speed. These people I had only read about on newspapers, and saw on TV. It was unbeliavable! I remember one day interviewing Irvin Khoza, the following day it was Jomo Sono, a week or so later it was Lucas Radebe! Months later, it was Shoes Moshoeu,Ted Dimitru, Tico-Tico Bucuane, Stanton Fredericks etc! Later, I contributed to Kickoff under Armien Harris. In 2007, I bumped onto an autobiography of Gabriel Batistuta.I gobbled it and later read about many football greats such as David Beckham, Maradona and Pele, and Madiba's boys Lucas Radebe and Mark Fish. I also later read Roger De Sa's autobiography Man of Action. Roger De Sa story was quite inspirational and more in context. Instinctively, something told me that there was something lacking in South Africa;the Doctor Khumalo autobiography. I tried to know more about Doctor Khumalo. I read many articles on him on the internet and I still felt I was not gratified. Most of his career, I watched him on TV as young boy in Botswana. I later also watched him live in South Africa although he was already in the twilight of his career. When I travelled to Zimbabwe in 2001, he was well known there. I had been puzzled by the manner in which he was famous especially in Botswana, Lesotho and Swaziland. In 2008, I decided that I would write a book about him. As early as 1993, I started keeping newspaper articles on Doctor Khumalo very safe in my room or locker. Some I kept under my bed. All my book notes of the 90's, the old soccer publications from Soccer News, Kickoff magazine to Soccer Laduma which I had been keeping away safe as a school boy suddenly became handy. I guess God was speaking to me all these years. Indiscernibly. In 2003, during Khumalo's farewell preparations, Doctor Khumalo's business manager Percy Adams had in one of the interviews said that Doctor Khumalo would write a book upon retirement. In 2008 or so, I approached and met Kaizer Chiefs about the idea, it proved quite difficult to come to an agreement because it was not their book or project. Kaizer Chiefs Head of Digital Media Kemiso Motaung and the Brand Manager Darra Caroll tried all they could to assist me. Doctor Khumalo and his Management Team were not keen to meet and talk. In 2010, when I personally asked Doctor Khumalo about the possibility of him and i writing and publishing his story together, he was not amenable to the idea. In fact, he indicated that someone in Pretoria was busy with it. I waited and waited. I genuinely wanted to do something to celebrate Doctor Khumalo. To say thank you to Doctor Khumalo in a more memorable and tangible way. Well, i accept that Okocha, Zidane and Ronaldinho were great dribblers and entertainers, but I think I did not see much of their game. Personally, I think Doctor Khumalo is probably the most skillful player i know after Jay Jay Okocha and Ronaldinho.I developed almost the same admiration for Junaid Hartley. But Junaid disappointed me a great deal with his personal indiscretions. For me, football is about giving the fans that smile. It's like that moment, that glorious moment we all look for when making love. It's important. Doctor Khumalo gave fans the smile more than anybody I have watched in the local game. He gave us the pleasure we sought to get from football. His big name and heart throb status made sure that females took notice of football. Doctor Khumalo is precisely what is lacking in South African football today. The poster boy of South African football. Teko Modise came very close to that stature until the 2010 world cup. Teko is an obscenely talented player. Teko reached superstardom with scintillating performances for Orlando Pirates and Bafana Bafana. He was the face of football for years leading up to the 2010 world cup. He was all over the billboards. He was on TV doing commercials for big brands like Sumsung and McDonalds. Teko Modise drove an Austin Martin amongst other luxury cars under his name. The media attention was always on him. He dated Lizelle Tabane, easily one of the most beautiful women in the continent. When the 2010 world cup came, with the world's eyes fully fixated on Teko Modise the superstar, he mysteriously failed to take the world cup by storm! Today Itumeleng Khune is the ultimate superstar, the poster boy of South African soccer. He is famous and is admired by both males and females. Siphiwe Tshabalala too, is enormously popular, a respected legend by all means but his reserved personality represents more of Shoes Moshoeu-humble, quiet and withdrawn. This personality limited the limelight on Shoes Moshoeu during his heyday. To some degree, its the same with Siphiwe Tshabalala. So, their impact is honestly not as weighty as Doctor Khumalo has been. Nigeria had this player in Jay Jay Okocha. Africa is poorer without this luxury footballer-the nonchalant one who makes people enjoy the beautiful game. Botswana has an exceptionally gifted Dirang Moloi, formerly with Vasco Da Gama in South Africa. He is the kind of player who is not in a rush. You could argue and say football has changed. Yes, drastically so. But isn't it a sport that is supposed to entertain people in the stands and those watching at home? Specially to please those who come with kids and spouses to get their money's worth. Boxing has also changed with billions of dollars in the fray but Floyd Mayweather still makes people enjoy the sport. People just want to have fun. Ok, we know they say its business. But football has always been a business. Club owners have always invested millions into the game. Patrice Motsepe is well known for putting astromical amounts of money in fooball. But before Motsepe, Zola Mahobe put a lot of money into Mamelodi Sundowns way back in the 80's. Goolam Allie, Dr Irvin Khoza, Kaizer Motaung, Dr Jomo Sono, John Comitis, Mike Mokoena and many others have ploughed incalculable amounts of money into football. Let's look for another excuse as to why football is so direct and so serious today. Why is South African football so boring today? There is no flair, nothing. Zane Moosa brought people to the stadium. The late Shakes Kungoane too. Rememeber the late Scara Ngobese? These days players with so much flair hardly start the game. They hardly even make it on the international stage. Why is that so? People criticize flair but they still wish to see more of Scara Ngobese! Don't they? Why is the whole world so critical of dribblers but would still give Doctor Khumalo so much love when they see him today! Who doesn't miss the skill of Thapelo Liau and Teboho Moloi? Who doesn't miss Donald Ace Khuse? I wish Alexi Lalas and Zinedine Zidane were still active today. Trust me when I say true African football supporters still wish Steve Lekoelea and Thabo Mooki were still playing soccer.

So, I took this decision not prompted by the thought of making money. It is important to have some sort of legacy upon which the next generation and foreign supporters could rely looking at the history of our football. I looked at a person like Nelson Mandela. South Africa took a deliberate decision to preserve and trumpet his legacy to the world. Many writers have also done the same, unauthorized. They have done this with or without him. This is over and above the books he has personally written. The most prominent of these books is the popular Long

Walk to Freedom. I wanted this book to be my personal tribute to Doctor Khumalo knowing that I shall never be able to thank him in a better way. Doctor Khumalo is now over 50 years old. This book is a timeless celebration of Doctor Khumalo. It's a timeless tribute to Doctor Khumalo, written by a Botswana citizen of South African extraction. I am not apologetic about celebrating a great man who has done so much for African football because I am African first and foremost. I consider myself a global citizen and Doctor Khumalo is a global hero. I must concede that this book does not solve the problems that exist in the general lack of respect for our own stars. It however gives a silver lining to many. I wish one day we could see a more in-depth story from the legend himself, straight up-written by Doctor Khumalo himself. Not only him but also many other legends writing their own stories for up coming generations to learn and know. Wouldn't the Benni McCarthy story by Benni McCarthy not inspire African boys? And Jomo Sono, Kaizer Motaung, Kalusha Bwalya, Tresor Mputu, Peter Ndlovu, Abedi Pele, Seydou Keita, Al Hadaary, Itumeleng Khune, Siphiwe Tshabalala, Fabrice Akwa, Tico Tico Bucuane, Dipsey Selolwane and others. How about they tell Africa and the world how they did it? The Teko Modise story (The Curse of Teko Modise) really opened many a player eyes especially on the subject of fame and fortune. Teko Modise speaks deeply from the heart on how Doctor Khumalo and Shoes Moshoeu inspired him as a youngster. To his credit, he has not disappointed his heroes. Today, Teko Modise is one of the most successful soccer players in history of the PSL.

The manner in which my father relayed Ace Ntsoelengoe's game to me was profound. When he narrated Ace Ntsoelengoe's game, I could see the game playing live in my eyes and mind. The passion was candid and immense. Unfortunately, I was never able to see Ace Ntsoelengoe play as I was too young. Again, there is very little on Ace Ntsoelengoe in the archives. This was my fear about Doctor Khumalo. I wanted to destroy this fear, once and for all. My son and his generation and those that follow him, should easily be able to find out and know what Doctor Khumalo did during his heyday. The time to celebrate Doctor Khumalo & Co is NOW. Ngoku! This book is a celebration of my star, my hero. There is no drama in this book. Nothing! I must therefore apologise in advance to those who expected drama and salacious stories about the life of Doctor Khumalo. On his 50th birthday, I wished Doctor Khumalo well, with a long text. I genuinely wished him another 50 years. His response was a simple but a bold THANK YOU. That response humbled me. Concise as it was.I will never forget it. I had and still have nothing adequate to thank Doctor Khumalo with except to publish this book in his honor. I hereby do, again wish Doctor Khumalo and family nothing but excellent health, more success, love and Peace. Thank you Mtungwa-ka-Mzilikazi-ka-Mashobane!!!

(1)

Meeting Doctor Khumalo

My first personal meeting with Doctor Khumalo was on September 25, 2005. I was in Cape Town, where it is not always easy to see soccer players, except for those who play for Cape Town clubs. Cape Town is the city where I have been based since 2002, although with negligible interruptions in between. Prior to my Matric studies, I had never lived in South Africa. While pursuing a law degree at the University of the Western Cape, my mind was already made up that I would permanently settle in South Africa thereafter. However, my history with South Africa goes beyond my academic pursuit. My paternal family is South African. My father was born and raised in Mabeskraal, a village 72 kilometers from Rustenburg. I therefore naturally developed a profuse interest in South Africa. However, I became particularly interested in South African football when I was about ten years old. Coincidentally, this was 1992, during the formation of the national team Bafana Bafana when the country was re-admitted into the international arena. As time went by, i developed serious interest in South African socio-economic and political dynamics, especially during the crafting of a new South Africa and the constitutional democracy we have today. So, on the day I would meet Doctor Khumalo, a Saturday morning in September 2005, I had just heard from my editor at 365 Digital, Anthony McLennan, that Doctor Khumalo would be in town for a skills competition organized by retail giant store Shoprite. I was at my apartment in Parow when I woke up a compatriot Lesego Sugar Motshabi. And off we rushed to Langa. I had not done any prior arrangement with Francois Hanekom, the organizer of the event. But I was quite fortunate. Hanekom was understanding enough to let me in together with Sugar, who had accompanied me. We were in Chris Hani hall in Langa Township. As expected, it was packed to the rafters. Idle township youths had come in numbers. Students too. Desperation and optimism, hunger and ambition filled that room. It was palpable, a truly pulsating atmosphere. The kind of commotion you see whenever Madonna visits Malawi on charity work. That was us at Chris Hani hall! It was unbelievable. Youngsters had filled that hall to the rafters to see their icon. Doctor Khumalo had effectively retired from playing soccer three years ealier. But if you were at that hall that Saturday morning, you would have thought that Doctor Khumalo was still an active professional player. The number of people who had come to see him told a compelling story. I found that *Kickoff* editor Zola Doda, was one of the judges of that competition. There was also popular professional football juggler Chris Njokwana, who was assisting Doctor Khumalo and Doda as judges sitting on the panel. I went to Doda and introduced myself. He said he was pleased to see me. He had probably seen my name at 365 Digital or bumped into me at local matches where I often went to cover PSL matches. I also went to greet Doctor Khumalo before I shook hands with Chris Njokwana. When I greeted Doctor Khumalo, Sugar was already all over us with a camera. I had set the camera for him to take pictures of me with the Kaizer Chiefs legend. Back then, the objective was not this book. The main objective was that I would be able to show off the pictures to my colleagues and friends at university. Most importantly, I wanted to show people back home in Botswana that I was the man. In Botswana, Doctor Khumalo was as big as Zlatan Ibrahimovich is in Sweden. Fortunately, in 2016, Somerset Gobuiwang and i flew to Sweden to attend the prestigious Gothia Cup. In Heden, right in the City of Gothenburg, I bumped into a hysterical group of soccer fanatics. One of the boys proclaimed to me that "Zlatan is God; Zlatan is Sweden!" The amount of energy that the small Swedish boy put into his words about Zlatan reminded me of the energy I witnessed on that day in 2005 at Chris Hani hall. The point in my case at Langa's Chris Hani hall was that, finally, I had an opportunity to meet and shake hands with one of the most popular sportsmen in Africa, Doctor Khumalo! I needed to show my parents and relatives back home in Botswana that indeed all our dreams could become a reality if we are patient enough. We had taken a taxi to Langa. For the first time in my first three years in Cape Town, I suddenly saw the need to go to a township which had become infamous for violent crime. I had to make my dream come true regardless of the danger. No matter what people and the media said about Langa. So, off we went. I guess I also wanted to dazzle my girlfriend at the time with pictures of myself with Doctor Khumalo. She knew in the literal sense what Doctor Khumalo meant to me as an individual. The pictures were more than important. But besides showing off, for what really? I did not understand! I would look at them very closely and see whether they were real. I was overwhelmed-star struck, as they say. I could not believe it. Towards the end of the competition, I had a quick but nervous chat with Doctor Khumalo. I knew I wanted to write something about Doctor Khumalo. Honestly, I did not know exactly what that would be.

"Hi, Mdokies. My name is Olebile Sikwane from Botswana. I wish to give you a proposal. How can one get it to you?" I asked.

"Can you please call me at the village-Chiefs headquarters on Monday or simply fax the proposal there? They will give it to me," Khumalo said, in the midst of Police who protected him.

For me, it was like I had won the lottery. What Doctor Khumalo had just said to me was sufficient. I had just had an opportunity to see Doctor Khumalo! I had just spent about three hours or so with Doctor Khumalo! Unbelievable! I was not able to say much to him as he was on the judges' table, but I would occasionally walk closer to them while he was talking to Zola Doda. I remember a group of local Kwaito dancers strutting their stuff there in the hall. Everybody seemed to be impressed with the dancers, including Doctor Khumalo himself. I jokingly asked him to tell his close friend and *Kwaito* Godfather Mdu Masilela that he should come to Cape Town and sign up the boys under his music stable. Khumalo looked at me and nodded his head with laughter, followed by, "I think so too, hey."

If you thought the ardent Masilo Machaka and the zealous Freedie Sadam Maake were the biggest Kaizer Chiefs supporters, it means you have not been to Botswana. There, in the dry and vulnerable Copper-Nickel mining town of Selibe Phikwe, was a youngster whose only dream was to work for Kaizer Chiefs one day, cynically just to see his childhood hero Doctor Khumalo. Immediately, from the young age of ten, I deliberately made Doctor Khumalo my focus, even on his farewell day to today in his retirement. My eyes have been fixated on Doctor Khumalo the brand, and Doctor Khumalo the legend, and Doctor Khumalo the person! What do you call that? Madness or fanaticism? A friend of mine Ntibi Kedikilwe, calls it hero worshipping. Maybe true, maybe wrong. For me, this is respect and appreciation of the talent that God has blessed us with. It comes from the bottom, the furthest part of my heart.

(2)

Dube Township, Soweto

Eliakim Khumalo was a top player during his heyday. He played for Kaizer Chiefs and Moroka Swallows in the early 70's and 80's. He married Mable Khumalo, a school teacher in Soweto. Mable gave birth to their first born, Fikile Khumalo, a bubbly beautiful daughter. Eliakim reportedly wished that his next child be a boy so that he could become a medical doctor in future-for he failed to be one himself. On 26 June 1967, a big healthy baby boy was born. Eliakim was reportedly ecstatic to welcome a "doctor" he had long wished for. They christened him Theophilus Doctorson Khumalo. He was the last born of the family, the only boy.

Growing up, Doctor Khumalo fantasized about becoming a Mohommed Ali or George Foreman since boxing was another popular craze in the townships of South Africa.Baby Jake Matlala, a former WBC world Champion was a rising star and inspired youngsters in Soweto including Khumalo and his contemporaries. They had also read and heard about Nelson Mandela. That Mandela liked boxing. Mandela was in prison undergoing his unpopular life sentence on Robben Island.The ANC icon had also trained Boxing in Soweto before his incarceration. Eliakim Khumalo was nearing the end of his career. It would appear that football had been inextricably embedded in the family. A genius had come into the family. A genius-not in medical terms, but a genius in the field of soccer, Theophilus Doctor Khumalo. Eliakim would not regret the choice made by his son.

It was never going to be easy. The youngster had been playing and perfecting his skills in the dusty wastegrounds of Soweto.His father Eliakim Pro Khumalo was already popular in

Soweto. A young Doctor Khumalo would often later watch him on television or at Orlando Stadium. Doctor Khumalo's parents were very close to him. They wanted the best for their only son. Their last-born child Doctor Khumalo. He was given guidelines withwhich to steer his life, influencing him in decision making but always allowing him the freedom of choice. He supported Kaizer Chiefs and opted soccer as second choice after his studies.

Doctor Khumalo went to Daliwonga High. This meant that to get into the school team you had to be known from the streets of Dube as a soccer player of amazing ability. He played with his friends like any other soccer great. That is how he discovered his talent. In fact, Bobby Motaung would later play a hugely positive role in discovering Doctor Khumalo. In the streets, the *shibobo's* and *tsamaya's* were the order of the day. These are townships tricks, loved by many. They make crowds go wild. They basically teaze the opponent. For example, *shibobo* is skillifully putting the ball through an opponent's legs. *Tsamaya* would simply mean a skill that sends the opponent away. Khumalo would outstand, and outstand he did. He had been watching Swallows and Chiefs from a very early age. The tricks he copied from his father's teammates and opponents had come right. In fact, most of them he would later admit, came naturally, due to consistent practice, curiosity and desire for perfection. He was almost there with the great players he watched at both Kaizer Chiefs and Moroka Swallows. Doctor Khumao had also played for Swallows Reserves before he joined Kaizer Chiefs. Clearly, his short-lived Swallows stint was a phenomenally grave misfortune for Moroka Swallows. He admits that as a youngster, the more he held onto his tennis ball the better his skills got. Doctor Khumalo's ball wizadry and artistry would later become apparent after making his professional debut for Kaizer Chiefs in 1987.

"I can only describe my upbringing in those days as smooth. I was born and raised in Dube, a place we used to call Freedom Centre because of the peace and tranquility which surrounded it. It was relatively untouched by the upheavels that were to characterise Soweto in the later half of the 70's. The adults were very much part of it, but as youngsters we would only learn of its social and political implications much later. We knew there were battles between the people and the police, but for us winning contests to see who would juggle the ball the longest, was more important."

At Daliwonga High, Khumalo proved beyond doubt that his football skills destined him for greater heights. At High School, he would come up against some of Soweto's best upcoming footballers notably Lesiba John Shoes Moshoeu of Namedi High. The school staff would predict that Doctor Khumalo would go places but never really imagined him captaining an overseas club in South America and later in the United States of America. Never mind Bafana Bafana and Kaizer Chiefs! He had been inspired by Chiefs' greats such as Ace Ntsoelengoe; Teenage Dladla; Shaka Ngcobo, Malombo Lichaba and Orlando Pirates' Jomo Sono who was a cult figure in South African football. Khumalo showed incredible talent, amazing ball skills and technique at an early stage. He used his extraordinary ball skills to lose his opponents. He had a very thin body physique and could not really pose a threat using his physique. But Doctor Khumalo used his brains. And fast. This is the thing he would say 15 years later when he had grown bigger in terms of the physical frame and age having caught up with him.

"As you grow a little older, the legs don't carry you, then you got to use the brain more, a little faster, that has been my strength. Remember I was never really a fast player,"

But at that stage he was still doing wonders week in and week out for the glamour club, Kaizer Chiefs. Pro Khumalo would go with little boy (Doctor) to football matches in Soweto when he was not playing and the youngster got excited and keener. During school tournaments, in 1985, Doc was spotted by (ironically) his friend and Kaizer Motaung's son, Bobby Motaung. Bobby had known Doctor Khumalo from way back during their school days and noticed the exceptional skills that Doctor Khumalo possessed.

Bobby Motaung tipped off his father Kaizer Motaung. A delegation of Kaizer Chiefs officials went to Pro Khumalo's house in Soweto.Pirates had also been notified about Doctor Khumalo's talent by a prominent supporter, Mamoipone. Unfortunately, Pirates only came later that evening when Motaung and his delegation had already secured the signature of the youngster. Pirates had missed out on what would perhaps be the most unmitigated scoop of their history since Jomo Sono's signature in the 70's. Ironically, Doctor Khumalo would become Pirates' biggest menace in big Soweto derbies that would follow over the years. In fact, just before he donned the black and gold jersey, Doctor Khumalo had briefly been under the watchful eye of Moroka Swallows' boss the late David Chabeli but at the under 14's. The under 14 group was dissolved as more focus was dedicated to the first team. That was when Doctor went back to school football played at a highly competitive level. Abe Matseng and Gabriel Tikkie Khoza took notice of the youngster and within a few days he was at Elkah Stadium in Rockville. He would meet a young tackling defender Rudolf Seale with whom he would become very close.

Lancelot Ntsie Maphike, Phil Mahaneloa and Brian Johnson were already there when Doctor Khumalo arrived at Chiefs. It is said that when Ntsie Maphike was promoted in 1986, Doctor Khumalo seemingly thought that his chance was now more probable. Indeed, he was promoted almost the same time with Ntsie Maphike and Rudolph Seale.It was a tough journey to the top. Doctor Khumalo had been under good guidance at home and watched strong and determined people like Ntsie Maphike do their stuff. But now, the dream was accompolished.

Eric September was another player who was at some stage close to Doctor Khumalo. They lived together with other Kaizer Chiefs players in a townhouse in Johannesburg. Doctor Khumalo was at the time, also studying for a Teacher's Diploma at Soweto College of Education. September, a lethal striker during his heyday, has sadly been serving a 27-year imprisonment after being convicted of murder of his own wife.

"I thought my turn would never come and I became despondent. I felt I should try my luck elsewhere," Khumalo said.

Without Ace, officials nearly snatched him but Amakhosi officials got wind of it. They had earmarked eight players including Doctor.

"I don't know how Chiefs' supporters got wind of it, but the kombi load of them came to my house. I was told in no uncertain terms I was not to going to betray them."

Khumalo started playing at Chiefs Reserves for some time. This is where he met his closest friend Teboho Moloi.

"Our dads took us to Ellis Park for a farewell game for Jomo Sono. It was the Chiefs oldies versus the Pirates oldies. I played against Doctor in a curtain raiser featuring the two clubs' junior sides. After that game in the players' lounge, Doc and I met each other, had a short chat and spoke about how we wished to make it to the next level where our fathers had been," Teboho Moloi said.

Doctor Khumalo had learned about greats such as De Stefani, Pele, Garrincha, and Johan Cryuff. However, names such as the phenomenal Jomo Sono, Ace Ntsoelengoe and the enterprising Ace Mnini made more sense to him. He would watch them play at Orlando Stadium in Soweto and his desire to become an even better player grew considerably. The struggle against Apartheid had reached its climax. Soweto, a black township just outside Johannesburg, was up in smoke. The police and black people fought against each other with the latter trying to defy the racist and discriminative white regime that ruled South Africa with an iron fist since 1948. Students in South Africa were clearly in a vehement mood. They totally resisted the use of Afrikaans as a medium of instruction in schools. There was a combination: a plethora of issues; low wages, insanitary housing, starvation, descrimination.

No voting rights! South Africa was in a quagmire and women were under immense hardship. Illiteracy and poverty as a result, became manifestly widespread. Freedom of movement in certain areas was prohibited. Whites could not marry blacks. Blacks could not marry whites. South Africa experienced the most brutal, inconsiderate and incompassionate rule in African history. Sanctions had been placed on the country by the international community. Fleeing the country was not very easy. It was not a pleasant experience altogether for a regular person in the streets.

(3)

The Debut, 1987

Doctor Khumalo made his professional debut in 1987 against traditional arch rivals Orlando Pirates.Imagine Theo Walcott of Arsenal making his debut against Tottenham Hotspurs. David Beckham or Ryan Giggs making his debut against Manchester United's traditional nemesis Manchester City. A young Raul Gonzalez of Real Madrid making a debut against Atletico Madrid or Barcelona.These are big games. These are not ordinary matches. In South Africa, Kaizer Chiefs vs Orlando Pirates match is the biggest event in local sports calendar. On the day, the position of either side on the log standings does not matter. Whether the other team is off form or on form is inconsequential. The previous match score between these arch rivals is null and void. What matters on that particular day is who actually wins the match. Whether Orlando Pirates win the league at the end of the season, their loss to Kaizer Chiefs will probably surpass the coveted league victory of that season. This is what I have observed over the years. The match draws attention across the African continent. People from Botswana take buses to Johanesburg to watch the Soweto derby. It's a serious excursion. In Botswana, Kaizer Chiefs is by far more popular than local clubs. It's an institution, a massive brand. It is the same in the region from Lesotho and Swaziland, Namibia to Zimbabwe and to some extent Zambia. They watch and follow South African football. The Soweto derby is generally watched by 48 countries across the world! Its huge. I must admit that the pattern may have changed significantly over the years especially with the advent of DSTV and Supersport, or rather the availability of English Premier League and LaLiga on our television sets. Fundamentally also because of social media. Also, credit must be given to local clubs of neighbouring countries. In the Botswana Premier League, i have observed a fierce rivalry between Township Rollers and Mochudi Centre Chiefs or Township Rollers against Gaborone United. This clash is a big day for supporters. Many supporters have decided to look to that rivalry. This has resulted into what seems like a peripheral interest in what goes on in the PSL in South Africa. In Zimbabwe, Highlanders of Bulawayo and Dynamos of Harare have also made their rivalry more interesting. While in Zambia, football has become so strong and competitive with the influence of mining corporations in football. The lucrative Supersport television deal in the Zambian Premier league was a cherry on top. Namibia may not be entirely disconnected from South Africa due to its inescapable colonial ties. Their football is trying to come off age. This is despite several interruptions of the league because of financial and corporate governance problems which engulfed their football in recent years. For Lesotho and Swaziland, most probably because of their geographical location within South Africa, it has therefore become difficult for them to ignore their strong interest in South African football. However, Matlama FC and Mbabane Swallows have both raised their hands as rallying points for their nations. Back to the Soweto derby. Supporters usually start to debate, argue and pontificate a month prior to the match. This continues even weeks after the game has been played. It will take time for the debate to settle. Fans and supporters, of both camps challenge each other. Some even bet while some go to the extent of sleeping outside the match venue, the night before the match. Television crew is always there two days prior to the match to avoid possibility of technical problems. It's just that crazy. It's an occasion. Its big business. The informal business thrives on this day. Big time.The political calendars of political parties change to accomodate the Soweto derby. Prominent politicians such as Julius Malema of the Economic Freedom Fighters and Bantu Holomisa of the United Democratic Movement religiously grace the Soweto derby. As far as I know, there has never been any match between the two giants that has not been broadcast live on television. Perhaps one needs to look at the history of the two clubs briefly. Kaizer Chiefs was formed by Kaizer Motaung-an Orlando Pirates player at the time who had just got back from the United States after a spell with Atlanta Chiefs. On arrival Motaung found that Orlando Pirates-his former club was now polarized by maladministration and disgruntlement. As a consequence of failed attempts at reconciliation, Motaung broke away with others following several futile meetings to broker the deadlock. Kaizer Chiefs was officially born in 1970, leaving angry Pirates supporters on the other side of Soweto. Pirates has a deep rooted, rich history in South Africa. They were the first black club to be formed as early as 1937.It seemed quite inconceivable that Kaizer Motaung would succeed with his rather rushed idea of forming his own club, at least to his father. He was with an intelligent and a clever group of friends which included a negotiator of note, the maverick team manager Ewert Nene. Kaizer Chiefs managed to attract most of the Orlando Pirates stars to the team. They became a fashionable group despite attempts by the league then to not have it registered. After registration, they started off well and had won several cups as early as 1974. In 1977, Chiefs had won the NPSL! Chiefs also won the Life Challenge Cup consecutively in 1971 and 1972.That stood them in good stead. The crowds took notice. People joined Chiefs in huge numbers. The club became copiously popular within Soweto.They had adopted Phefeni, a location in Soweto as their place of birth. They later adopted "Phefeni Glamour Boys" as their tag line. Today, Kaizer Chiefs is a monsterous institution with a registered and card-carrying membership exceeding 16 million supporters!Doctor Khumalo made his debut at Ellis Park in 1987. It was an Iwisa Cup Spectacular event. He was still at Daliwonga High School then and a lot of noise had been made up for this match. Teboho Moloi, his close friend up to this day-was in the opposition team, Orlando Pirates. The late Ted Dumitru, an American citizen of Romanian origion was in charge of Kaizer Chiefs. Ted Dumitru had Doctor Khumalo on the bench for this encounter. Kaizer Chiefs had the likes of Ace Ntsoelengoe, Trevor Mthimkhulu, Scara Thindwa, and Howard Freeze in their team. Icons and Legends!

Doctor Khumalo made a debut on that day with Kaizer Chiefs pipping Pirates 2-1. Scara Thindwa and Trevor Mthimkulu scored for Chiefs.

Khumalo relates January 17, 1987 with nostalgia.

"I could not believe it when Ted gave me a chance. I had butterflies in my stomach. Ace Ntsoelengoe was there; he said you go boy. Grab this opportunity and I did just that. I never looked back. It was a defining moment that I will never forget. With about 60.000 supporters looking at this skinny 19 year old playing for Chiefs against Pirates-a team so rich in history. It was remarkable. In fact, my dad had been against the idea of playing me against Pirates on my first professional match."

Two months later, Chiefs met Pirates in a National Soccer League encounter in which Doctor Khumalo opened the score line, giving Chiefs a lead in the 41st minute. It was Ernest Makhanya's penalty that would cancel Chiefs' lead before Howard Freeze gave Chiefs a winner in the 76th minute. In this match, it appears that Doctor Khumalo had worked hard but smart to endear himself to the hordes of Chiefs supporters. This is how a monumental journey started. It was a great journey indeed. Doctor Khumalo went on to achieve a historic record over a period of 15 years of active career with Chiefs. Doctor Khumalo holds the record having played 397 matches, scoring 75 goals in the gold and black of Kaizer Chiefs.Tshabalala was very close, but left for Turkey having played 342 matches, scoring 55 goals. Itumeleng Khune is the only player who looks set to equal or supass this match record if he does not move to another club. I wish him well in both possibilities.

(4)

Bafana Bafana, 1992

The beginning of the history of Bafana Bafana would not be complete without mention of the name Doctor Khumalo. It was against the Indomitable Lions of Cameroon, on 7th July 1992, at King's Park Stadium in Durban when Doctor Khumalo took an 82nd minute penalty that marked South Africa's first ever goal after the country's readmission to world football. When the first squad was assembled, Doctor Khumalo was not part of it! He forced his way into the team during a League Select Eleven against Bafana Bafana in a friendly match that prepared the Bafana team for its first official match. South Africa suffered a 4-1 Peter Ndlovu inspired drubbing by Zimbabwe in Harare in a match that saw the famous Doctor Khumalo being nicknamed the 'Nurse' by a Zimbabwe player. Bafana would then suffer another 4-0 defeat against Nigeria in a World Cup Qualifier in Lagos, and later in an away friendly international fixture to Mexico in Los Angeles, (4-0). Mark Fish made a debut in this away defeat.

"We should never have gone and played there. The team morale was low and we were up against a team that had just qualified for the 94 World Cup. We did not stand a chance. The less said about that game the better."

Stanley Screamer Tshabalala, the first Bafana Bafana coach had been released after a widely publicized incident against leading and respected veteran journalist Sy Lerman. Peruvian-born mentor Augusto Palacios was brought on board for the United States tour. But the team's first away victory was against minnows Botswana in Gaborone. Botswana football fans have an amazing passion for the game of football. However, many in Botswana thought that the match would be a walkover by their all-powerful neighbor South Africa.Until 1998, Botswana had no local television station. Therefore, the country relied enormously on South African Broadcasting Corporation (SABC) which consequently meant that Doctor Khumalo and his team Kaizer Chiefs became excessively popular in Botswana. I became a victim of that absolute consumption as a youngster like many of my contemporaries in Botswana and elsewhere in Africa. Almost every soccer youngster growing up in Botswana aspired to be like Doctor Khumalo or even better. Doctor Khumalo is often seen in South African magazines and papers which hit shelves with amazing regularity in Botswana. It didn't end there. South African television was the only form of pastime in the evening which we had back then. This applied across the region. Back in the day, it was called CCV-TV. Today it is called SABC. Doctor Khumalo became a major hit amongst Batswana especially in the early 90s until the late 90's. He was a social craze amongst the people. Young girls also had him on their book covers. Their room walls would be painted with his pictures. My aunts also had him on their wardrobe doors. My female cousins had him on their bedroom walls. The school girls we liked at school had him all over their books! I also had his poster on my school locker! He was a major sex symbol and still is too many female fans. He was to us black people what Denzel Washington and Mohommed Ali are to the Afro American community in the United States. Doctor Khumalo served as an example of not only sophistication but success for ambitious young black men in South Africa. It was the same phenomenon in Southern Africa. Since the early 90s when I started following soccer in South Africa, there has never been a more famous sports man than Doctor Khumalo in South Africa. I am not sure if Itumeleng Khune, Teko Modise, Siphiwe Tshabalala, Lucas Radebe, Francois Piennar, Makhaya Ntini, Benni McCarthy, Hashim Amla or Brian Habana have reached the popularity levels that Doctor Khumalo reached in his heyday. If there is one, I would like to know that sportsman. I have been living in South Africa for nearly 15 years now. I have been following Doctor Khumalo since 1992. He has truly been the golden boy to South Africa from all sporting, gender and racial divide. One day listening to the mercurial Azania Mosaka on Metrofm, she was talking about an extremely talented musician, popular and well received. However, according to

Azania, the musician lacked the star gravitas and stature that Beyonce, Rihanna or Jennifer Lopez generally command. Now this is exactly my point. South Africa has had very great superstars. But there has always been something enigmatic about Doctor Khumalo. This Azania Mosaka analogy is compelling. I see it every day. I accept almost immediately that the likes of Mark Fish, the late Shoes Moshoeu, Benni McCarthy and Lucas Radebe were superstars, and are still famous today. They have been all over the world. They have been markedly successful in their own right. However, they never quite achieved the star status and popularity that Doctor Khumalo commanded and still does locally. Lucas Radebe and Benni McCarthy in particularly, have been mega stars abroad. Rightly so. McCarthy won the Champions League with Porto under Jose Mourinho in 2004. Lucas continues to be a lord at Leeds United with numerous personal accolades. These two legends are also catergorized in the league of the super rich. They are world superstars. I understand and accept that they played outside South Africa for the longest period of their careers. But back home here in South Africa, they have not achieved equal adoration and they are yet to receive the kind of love South Africa gives Doctor Khumalo. So, there is just something about Doctor Khumalo. It appears that the majority of soccer people in South Africa and the region naturally love Doctor Khumalo. It may well be because Doctor Khumalo played his football in South Africa for at least 15 years of the 17 years of his career. During this time, these other greats such as Quinton Fortune, Benni McCarthy, Eric Tinkler, Shoes Moshoeu and Lucas Radebe spent generally a decade and a half or more abroad. But let's agree that Doctor Khumalo just had that thing about him. In Zimbabwe for example, Peter Ndlovu was extremely popular. He became the first black African to play in the English Premier League. That was a major achievement. Peter Ndlovu is still the biggest symbol of football in Zimbabwe. This is despite the fact that Peter Ndlovu left Zimbabwe at the age of 16 years for England where he played for clubs notably Coventry City and Sheffield Wednesday in his 14-year long career in Europe. Peter Ndlovu has hardly lived in Zimbabwe again. However, his name remains inscribed in the hearts and memories of many Zimbabweans to date. Benjamin Mwariwari and Knowledge Musona are yet to take his crown. The legendary Samuel Eto'o left Cameroon at the age of 14 years. Today he is a god of Cameroon despite the fact that he has never lived in Cameroon again. Why no one has taken the crown off Doctor Khumalo still buffles me? Doctor Khumalo has been incalculably fortunate on and off the field.

In a match at National Stadium in Gaborone 1993, Doctor Khumalo was marked by a talented leftback, Nephtally 'Scara' Kebalepile and no-nonsense tackler Rapelang Raizor Tsatsilebe. Nephtally Kebalepile became a household name in Botswana after that match. Doctor Khumalo played ok. He had support in the same opposition he was playing against. He had managed to beat both Scara Kebalepile and Raizer Tsatsilebe at different times in the match. After that match, Raisor Tsatsilebe was invited for trials in Cape Town with Lightbodys' Santos as an acknowledgement that he had done fairly well in that encounter.

John Shoes Moshoeu was a debutant on that day in Gaborone. Shoes Moshoeu was another extremely talented and hardworking Chiefs player who made history scoring on debut. Fast running lefback Rudolph Seale completed the score line to give the favorites a 2-0 win over Botswana. The Botswana match was a preparatory friendly against the mighty Nigerians five days later in Johannesburg. In 2012, President Thabo Mbeki reminded us in a nostalgic speech delivered in Gaborone at the Sir Ketumile Masire Foundation, that the match was not just a friendly international but sought to acknowledge Botswana's role in dismantling Apartheid.

"a few of us drove from Johannesburg to witness this historic but friendly game, which I think the Botswana team lost, but whose intent and spirit had very little to do with sporting prowess and everything to do with what i have said about Botswana serving as the bridge in the historic transition from Apartheid to African liberation," Mbeki said.

It is common course that Botswana hosted Nelson Mandela in Lobatse during his short-lived exile in the diamond rich country in 1960. However, for Thabo Mbeki and his comrades, Botswana served as a gateway to the Western world. In 1962, Mbeki and his comrades took an aircraft in Gaberones to Tanganyika en-route to London where he would link up with the great Oliver Tambo. Tambo was ANC President who spent well over three decades shuttling between Europe and the world spreading ANC gospel. For Bafana Bafana players, this match was important to demonstrate their dominance over their lowly rated neighbours. Afterall, South Africa had not been eligible to play in the international space due to sanctions by the international community. South Africa wanted to prove a point to the world that they too could compete, with anybody. Being banned from the international community meant that South Africa was banned from all FIFA activities. This is despite the fact that South Africa was one of the founding members of FIFA!

"The training had begun straight after the Super Bowl final. We stayed in camp until the game in January, so we were super fit. We spent so much time together and it made us feel like a family. For the first time, I felt like playing for my country. It was a new coach (Augusto) and it was like a new beginning. It made me really play well," Khumalo said.

The truth is that the Botswana match saw Shoes Moshoeu put on a very good performance. The rivalry between the two nations started here as evidenced by the subsequent matches. Except for the famous quarterfinal penalty shoot out win in a COSAFA cup in 2006 aside, Botswana still remains in the shadow of South Africa in the eight encounters they have met thus far. The sad thing for Doctor Khumalo's fans in Botswana is that he never played against Botswana again except when LCS Gunners qualified for CAF Champions League and were pitted against Kaizer Chiefs. Amakhosi drubbed the Lobatse side 5-1 in aggregate.

"In the first leg there, there were fans all over our bus. I was at the back and I could hear what they said. They were enthusiastic and really fancied their chances. We beat them 2-1."

Gunners then went to face a determined Kaizer Chiefs at a packed Rand stadium in the 2nd leg in Johannesburg. Doctor Khumalo worked his magic. He did all the show boating and all the *shibobos* with a lifeless Gunners wishing for the end. Chiefs comfortably won the match 3-0.

"I wanted to show them the difference between the two teams. We were just too strong for Gunners.I think we scored all the three goals in the first 30 minutes. I played a part and I did my thing the whole game."

The match against Nigeria would come six days later after the Gunners match. Doctor Khumalo put a very solid performance just like all the other lads. George Dearnely gave Bafana a much-needed goal which was not given after the referee mistakenly ruled Doctor Khumalo to be offside. However, the replay showed that Khumalo wasn't interfering with play. The match ended 0-0. South Africa's World Cup dreams were almost remote by now.

South Africa went on to play against Congo in Pointe Noire.That was the same month of January.Africa is one big continent with its very unique problems. Unless you are in Southern Africa or North Africa, logistically, Africa is not easy to navigate in terms of travel and hospitality. Steel strong defender Mark Fish could write a book about events which took place in Pointe Noire, prior and during the match. Mind games and tricks play out deliberately to destabilize opponents. There is a reason for this attitude. Infrastructure wise, African countries are simply behind the big five; South Africa, Morocco, Algeria, Tunisia and Egypt. Congo Brazzaville is certainly one of the most unfortunate countries in Africa.

"It was an excellent result up there.Harold Legodi scored.We were getting used to travelling to different countries but the problem was the pitch.It was in shocking condition which made it difficult to play on.It was the best trip I've been on since I was with the national team.After the game we had a party in the hotel.Every South African who was there, came to celebrate with us,"Doctor Khumalo told Kickoff.

But when a talented player like Doctor Khumalo is happy, he would deliver a splendid performance week in and week out for the team. The match against Brazil at FNB comes to my mind. What a night! That 3-2 match result hurt most people. Doctor Khumalo was all over Brazil. He suffocated Rivaldo. His corner kick was converted by Phil Masinga. Doctor Khumalo was totally in charge. He even scored a scotcher, a volley from outside the box giving Bafana Bafana a 2-0 lead against Brasil a half time. This substitution seemed to be a ghastly mistake by Coach Clive Barker. It opened a vacuum. Rivaldo and Brazil took control of the match. Flavio scored the first goal before the great Rivaldo himself scored the equalizer. Bebeto clinically and spectacularly finished Bafana Bafana off with a beautiful scissor kick two minutes before the final whistle. 3-2! At final whistle Clive Barker, the man who was loved by all was booed off the field. There was no explanation about Doctor Khumalo's substitution until recently.

"In that moment, all seemed possible, but then Doc delivered a killer blow; he was buggered and didn't think he would be able to finish the game. He suggested he be substituted,"Barker writes.

Barker went on.

"I was angry and, out of character in my dealing with him, I had a go at him to suck it up because we needed him. My ego was getting the better of me. I did not listen to someone I should have."

This Brazil match was one of the defining moments of Clive Barker's career. This Doctor Khumalo substitution matter against Brasil hurt Cliver Barker. Permanently so.

"Doctor had run himself to the point of exhaustion in the first half and he was being honest with me, trying to warn me that he was going to be a liability. Against teams like Brasil, attack is sometimes the best form of defence and we were about to lose our attacking kingpin.'

According to Clive Barker, as coach, he should have done something to secure the 2-0 score line.

''I should have made the change at half time, but i imagined the response of that expectant crowd if we had emerged after the break without Doctor in the line up."

However, it is different when your most talented player is not happy. As coach or supporter, you are not going to get the best out of him. I watched South Africa play Mauritius in Johannesburg. It was clear that something was bothering Doctor Khumalo's mind. Bafana Bafana did not have a good game against one of the perennial minnows of African football.

"I had a bad game but things happened before the match that really disturbed me and I went into the game with a negative mind. The guys weren't happy with the money they were getting. Then, there was Chris Hani's death and we didn't know if we were going to play, so it was difficult to concentrate," Doctor Khumalo said.

After the Mexico defeat in Los Angeles, Palacios was sacked. In came a less known Clive Barker. Barker had been a fairly successful coach at club level. He had been with Durban City with whom he won league titles in 1982 and 1983 respeictvely. He had, and still has not coached any of the big three clubs in South Africa. He has never managed Moroka Swallows, Kaizer Chiefs,Mamelodi Sundowns, and Orlando Pirates. Clive Barker has always been synonymous with Amazulu-a top Durban club that has had a fair share of both ups and downs in its rich history, both as a traditional pride for Kwazulu-Natal and the Zulu nation. Amazulu are very strong in support in Kwazulu-Natal and Barker would certainly not have a problem with pressure at national level. In the 80's and 90's, Amazulu were very strong winning cups and attaining respectable league positions. In 1992, Barker led Usuthu who strolled to a famous 3-1 Coca Cola victory over a star studded Kaizer Chiefs. Barker has also been seen as some kind of a messiah by Usuthu owners. He has parted ways with them on a number of occasions only to be recalled, on many ocassions.Amazulu have recently had a history of relegation. However they are back in the elite league through a purchase of Thanda Royal Zulu franchise status. Whenever Amazulu were in trouble, Barker would be called up to help out. The truth is that Barker loves Amazulu too much. His relationship with the club is manifestly reciprocal.

Upon taking over at Bafana Bafana, Barker made it clear that Doctor Khumalo would form part of his team going on record that the skinny Kaizer Chiefs fan favorite was an ''intelligent crafty player who makes the team play.''

"No coach would leave him out of the national team, let's be honest. Would you? If you don't want to keep your job you can leave out the most creative player in the country," Barker said.

Khumalo would go on to play a pivotal role in the Bafana set up the during the entire Clive Barker era which lasted six years. Besides Ted Dumitru, Doctor Khumalo probably owes Clive Barker a higher debt of gratitude than he does any other coach in his entire career. Off the field, Clive Barker and Doctor Khumalo formed a great deal of relationship. Today in their own separate ventures, they still remain very close. Barker's profile as a club coach was just ok. At Bafana Bafana, he was too good. Barker always picked a strong team. As early as June, i would be able to predict Bafana team that would play a match in November. Andre Arendse, Sizwe Motaung, David Nyathi, Lucas Radebe Mark Fish, Neil Tovey, Eric Tinkler, Doctor Kumalo, John Moshoeu, Phil Masinga and Helman Mkhalele. Mark Williams, Shaun Bartlett, Linda Buthelezi, Augustine Makalakalane and John Moeti would form part of his bench. This was a consistent team, called from all parts of the world to come home and give

South Africa a smile. South Africa would soon become a formidable force under Clive Barker. They went on to win the 1996 Africa Cup of Nations that the country hosted. Barker instantly became a hit with supporters. His players became very popular that in most cases a substitute would be given a rapturous welcome even when nobody understood the purpose of that change. Another thing noticeable about Barker is that he was a great motivator. Tactically, not the most astute of coaches, but a gifted team builder whose philosophy was premised on unity and discipline, on and off the field. Interestingly, Clive Barker announced years before Neil Tovey retired, that Lucas would be succeed Tovey as national team captain. Radebe was then an emerging centre back in the English Premiership playing for Leeds United. Clive Barker just simply knew how to build a team of leaders. For him, this transition was natural and organic. Lucas Radebe was the natural successor to Neil Tovey, South Africa's most respected captain who had just led South Africa to the 1996 Afcon victory.

Barker's first assignment would be against Zimbabwe. Zimbabwe was a powerful force then. Then, they were second only to Zambia in Southern Africa by strength. Zimbabwe had more players overseas than South Africa. The likes of the Ndlovu brothers namely Peter, Madinda, and Adam Ndlovu. There was Vitalis Takawira, Benjamin Nkonjera and the popular Bruce Grobelaar of Liverpool were some of the overseas based players who the Warriors had in their star-studded line up.

Barker's line up was quite obvious and easily predictable. Steve Crowley, Sizwe, Nyathi, Lucas Tovey, Khumalo, Shoes etc. The team was talented but would they hold Zimbabwe? Khumalo had formed a very deadly combination with Shoes Moshoeu who had just moved to Turkey. Shoes Moshoeu was an incredibly talented player. He was quick. He possessed unrivalled dedication and passion for the game. Tactically, a better player than most of the Bafana midfielders. Shoes Moshoeu was a fine player; a supremely intelligent midfielder. He, unlike most players, had the requisite pace and balance necessary for modern football. Shoes

Moshoeu would quietly go on with his work throughout the match without much fanfare. The results of his hard work were palpable.

He broke the transfer fee record when Kaizer Chiefs bought him for R250,000 from Giant Blackpool. He later moved to Turkey after a few matches for Amakhosi.He broke the South African all-time record when he was signed by Fernabache at a $2.4 million fee. Shoes Moshoeu preferred direct play which meant going forward all the time. He had a fantastic passing ability, aided by incredible work rate which meant that he would regularly go back to help his team when under pressure. This is something that both Doctor Khumalo and the silky skilled Zane Moosa lacked. Shoes Moshoeu is probably the oldest player to have played in South Africa's Premier League at the age of 41. He would also captain Bafana Bafana on several occassions in his 73 appearances-a record broken by Shaun Bartlett who would later be surpassed by Bafana Bafana strongman Aaron Mokoena, the acrobatic Itumeleng Khune and the legendary Siphiwe Tshabalala.

Doctor Khumalo was blessed with accurate and extraordinary passes. He had an unmatched dribbling ability reminiscent of Nigeria's Jay Jay Okocha and Egypt's Abdel Satta Sabry.Clive Barker went public about his admiration for Doctor Khumalo! He cited the player as a unique, unselfish and crafty player who would be crucial to any team. Clive Barker further went on to say that he planned Bafana matches around Doctor Khumalo. Clive Barker emphasised to his players to play balls to Doctor Khumalo especially when the going got tough. Strikers who failed to capitalise on Doctor's precise passes would kiss the national team goodbye. Doctor Khumalo 's strength was premised on his incredible skill and guile. Doctor Khumalo was a gifted midfielder in the true meaning of the word.

Former Leeds United Striker Phil Masinga and Wolverhaptom's Mark Williams became major beneficiaries of Doctor's passes by converting them into goals. In August 1997, against Congo Brazaville,Khumalo cleverly intercepted a ball that landed into Masinga's feet. Masinga unleashed a powerful scotcher outside the 18-box to give South Africa its most famous goal ever-that goal qualified South Africa for its maiden world cup. In Botswana, we called it *Siyaya*. That goal qualified South Africa for its first World Cup ever in France 1998. Doctor Khumalo became a massive, phenomenal public hero. Masinga on the other hand, was always under tremendous crowd scrutiny whenever he donned the national jersey. Fans would boo him for unknown reasons whenever he was in possession of the ball. On this day, Phil Masinga had sent a clear message. The fans were happy for Bafana. They gave Phil Masinga intense love this time around. Doctor Khumalo would also recieve compliments and accolades from all angles and spheres of life. He was a generous player who gave players an opportunity to score and shine. True. Doctor Khumalo did not want all the glory attributed to himself alone, fans opined.

Like Teenage Dladla and Ace Ntsoelengoe, Doctor Khumalo was the man. He commanded admiration,respect and adoration. People just truly liked Doctor Khumalo.No other Southern African team had achieved this feat. South Africa was the emerging football force in Africa. Zimbabwe had not qualified. Zambia had lost a powerful team in an aircraft crash on the coast of Gabon. They were sadly rebuilding despite doing well in the 1994 Afcon losing 2-1 to a star-studded Nigeria led by the all powerful Rachidi Yekini.South Africa had just come out of world sanctions which also included non participastion at international events. What South Africa achieved was a remarkable feat. SAFA President at the time, Solomon Stix Morewa was full praise of the success. The players looked very happy. The fans were obviously thrilled.

That meant that the whole Southern Africa region would be behind South Africa in its quest to qualify for France 98. The SABC has always dominated households in Africa, especially in the Southern African region. Advertising of many goods in the region carried Bafana Bafana players. They became popular. South Africa is the supreme trade partner in the SADC region. The goods would have Bafana Bafana players with Doctor Khumalo being the most fortunate of them all. He appeared more. These were the stars, the cool guys. Soccer fans liked the type of play they dished out. The nation liked the type of results they garnered. Stadiums were always full. People wanted to see Doctor Khumalo, Shoes Moshoeu, Mark Williams, Lucas Radebe, Shaun Bartlett, Helman Mkhalele, Mark Fish, Sizwe Motaung and others. There were mavericks in the team like Augustine Makalakalane. Makalakalane was a supremely gifted midfielder. I believe that Makalakalane was generally largely misunderstood as a player in South Africa. He had his trade mark white boots. He lived and played his football in Swirtzerland. He was already advanced at the time. Makalakalane faced incredible scrutiny with his innovative hairstyles and flamboyant white boots. The fans waited with anxiety to see the latest hairstyle Shoes Moshoeu would be sporting on match day. He too had a great deal of sophistication about him. He was sophisticated, based in Turkey at the time. Eric Tinkler was based in Portugal. He had his trade mark tinted hairstyle which he still carries to this day as a top-flight coach.

People truly liked and rallied behind the Bafana Bafana team. During all this euphoria, Doctor Khumalo built his name and brand into a cult. The media catapulted this name religiously to the people. He was all over. Doctor Khumalo became a phenomenally accepted brand. He was without doubt South Africa's most famous black person after Nelson Mandela. There is a naughty story that the first time Mandela met Doctor Khumalo, he said "oh, this is Doctor Khumalo? I want to be famous like you." He had a prolific following both young and old. Black and white. Male and female. Good news for a player who just loved doing tricks on the field of play to entertain the supporters and fans who had come in big numbers. A player who would go out there to embarass his opponents in a sublime way, putting the ball through the opponent's legs. A player who would often score unbelievable goals for his team. Doctor Khumalo liked doing beautiful things on the field of play. He would try all his best to score a beauty. In fact, in a situation where he just had to put the ball into the back of the net, more often than not, he would wait for the goalkeeper or defence to recover and round them all over again before slotting the ball into the net. I saw that at one of the derbies. Unfortunately, it cost Kaizer Chiefs a win when he took the ball over the post when he had only Williams Okpara to beat and score. But Doctor Khumalo played with a smile which is important in football. Ronaldinho also had lots of fun in his game, with a big smile. Samuel Eto'o too, is well known for playing with that ubiquitous smile. This is for the love of the game. The beautiful game.

Africa's most authoritative soccer publication Kickoff Magazine, read throughout the African continent did a survey in the late 90's which indicated that Doctor Khumalo was the most famous sportsman in South Africa. He polled 48% of the votes, pipping the late boxing great Baby Jake Matlala, Bolton Wanderers' Mark Fish, cricketer Hansie Cronje and Orlando Pirates fast forward Jerry Sikhosana. In 2004, Doctor Khumalo was voted 62nd in the Top 100 Greatest South Africans in a nationwide public poll, run through a popular tv show hosted by Noleen Maholwana Sangcu and Denis Beckett. Nelson Mandela and IT billionaire Mark Shuttleworth were some of the people who topped this list.

To many of us, Doctor Khumalo is to South Africa what George Weah is to Liberia. George Weah defied all odds in world football, representing a country with a painful history. George Weah became a superstar despite all odds. Today, George Weah is President of his country, the Republic of Liberia. Doctor Khumalo was to football in South Africa, what Michael Jordan was to basketball in the United States and elsewhere. I would not be incorrect to suggest that Doctor Khumalo was to South Africa what Zinedine Zidane was to the French nation. A little God? Most probably. Doctor Khumalo would do no wrong on the field. He would not be in the papers for bad behavior neither. He would be in the papers doing commercials. Doing charity work. Sometimes chilling out in *the township* with musicians like Mdu Masilela and Mandoza. His public confidence and stature grew rapidly. He manifestly relished the fact that he was South Africa's favourite son. Everything and anything he touched turned into gold. Money and fame came. Fast and furious. Big things followed. More national caps and goals. Trophies, endorsements and commercials. Big interviews and appearing in magazine covers.

Recognition after recognition. Award after another. But Doctor Khumalo being Doctor Khumalo, the son of Mable and Pro Khumalo, kept his head and ears down.

While he was never a prolific scorer, it was the manner in which he dictated play and made things happen that really set him apart from his peers. His creative mind set him apart from many a footballer. Doctor Khumalo's football antics made him a marvel to watch. He was truly a class act. Samuel Eto'o admits that Doctor Khumalo inspired him.

"Doctor Khumalo was a great player. I watched him play while I was young, and I just wanted to be like him. For his talent, he should have played in Europe."

He would mesmerize defenders on the line. He would do his famous "roll over" on the ball. He would drive the ball in that lackadaisical Zinedine Zidane attitude. Like he was not interested. Like he was not on the ball with authority. Supporters liked it because he embarrassed opponents when they approached him unprepared. He however played balls forward. Doctor Khumalo, unlike midfield genius Donald Ace Khuse, hardly played the ball backwards. He liked unleashing long passes to strikers like Mark Williams who would not mind beating defenders for pace before rounding the goalkeeper to score. Shaun Bartlett and Phil Masinga often converted these passes with ease as well at the national team.

There is no doubt that Fani Madida, Shane McGregor, Phil Masinga, Mark Williams and Shaun Bartlett were great beneficiaries of Doctor Khumalo's intelligent passes. They finished very well with precision. The rule was that, if you could not convert them. You have kissed Bafana Bafana goodbye. In Setswana township parlance *"o a tshola"*; in Township lingo, we said Doctor Khumalo "dished" passes. That meant that the recipient simply had to 'eat' (score) in simple terms; tap in to goal. A true soccer supporter would admit that Khumalo was a class act. When it came to Doctor Khumalo's skills and talent, club affiliation was not a factor.

Fans and supporters, friends and foes across South African club divide, generally agree that Doctor Khumalo was a truly gifted player by any standards.

(5)

AFCON,1996

"An extremely alert and committed Andre Arendse in goals, massively dedicated defence led By Neil Tovey, Lucas, Fish, Sizwe and Nyathi, the midfield work horses in Linda and Eric Tinkler, the flair and brilliance of a younger Shoes Moshoeu, and the most talented of all South African players, Doctor Khumalo, Shaun, Phil and Mark leading the attack it was impossible to let our fans down on our own soil."

These are the words of coach Clive Barker. Barker is the man who led Bafana Bafana to their most triumphant victory to date. He does not beat about the bush about Doctor's influential role during his tenure at the helm.

Being named the hosts of the 2010 FIFA world cup was historic and memorable. Another, maybe even more memorable football moment in the lives of many soccer loving people,was the African Nations Cup that South Africa hosted and won in 1996. Kenya was initially earmarked to host this prestigious football tournament but was accordingly denied the right to host due to their government's failure to prepare for the show. South Africa would automatically take over from the East Africans as a more suitable alternative. South Africa, because of its world class infrastructure, logistical connectivity and other economic factors would naturally be the most convenient host. The rights to host the World Cup 2010 in South Africa were awarded following intense lobbying including bringing the retired Nelson Mandela and the retired archbishop Desmond Tutu into the global campaign. This also meant a great deal of travelling by Dr Jordaan and Dr Khoza. South Africa then hosted a magnificent World Cup, by far a truly outstanding piece. Sadly, six years after the event, allegations that the rights to host the 2010 World Cup were bought emerged! Highly respected writer Ray Hartley reveals in his book, *The Big Fix; How South Africa stole the 2010 world cup*. These allegations dampened the claim that South Africa had the universal ability to bid,compete and win fairly. However, in the 1996 Afcon, the rights were simply given to South Africa. Understandably so because Kenya had been struck out as hosts due to their own incapacity. That South Africa is by and large more advanced than any other African country is without doubt. In fact South Africa is more advanced than most of Eastern Europe in terms of infrastructure and economic strength. The World Bank and the International Monetary Fund catergorize South Africa in the class of newly industrialized nations alongside Brasil, Russia, India and China. The infrastructure in South Africa is astonishingly world class, with some of the best hotels in the world. It has a sophisticated transport network and a host of other amenities which placed her in a supreme position not only to host the 1996 Afcon but also the 2010 world cup. But there were compelling reasons why South Africa had to host the world cup in 2010. Following the snub in 2006, where a New Zealander ran away with a vote that gave Germany the rights, Africa and FIFA top brass were deeply bruised and visibly hurt. For the Afcon 1996, it was imperative that South Africa had to host the Afcon.President Mandela was preaching reconciliation,fresh from prison and fresh from the 1994 electoral victory. For the 2010 world cup,in his book The Big Fix; Ray Hartley discloses the intrigue that won South Africa the rights to host the world cup. It is an expose' of people who amassed wealth illicitly using everything they could use to guarantee that success. Hartley shows how money was diverted from its intended use to guarantee that South Africa hosted the 2010 world cup by hook or crook. How South Africa got to host the World Cup may still be subject to investigation but the manner in which the World Cup was delivered was exceptional. The 2010 world cup remains the most successful World Cup in history, in terms of profit made.

One of the indirect influencial reasons for the 1996 Afcon surprise was probably because of the country's ultimate long walk to freedom. Nelson Mandela had just been inaguarated as

President two years ago. The tournament would help strengthen perceptions about South Africa. Africa's most advanced economy whose people were deeply divided was an irony President Mandela couldn't stomach. These people, without doubt-needed these matches and tournament for reconcillation purposes. This tournament truly merged South Africa's racial blurs into a united rainbow nation envisaged by those who had fought against oppression. It was a monumental success on all spheres, terms and aspects.

Clive Barker had been building a spirited and enthusiastic bunch of players that was eager to showcase their talent to the outside world. A team now with a sizeable influence of players plying their trade in top overseas leagues in England,Turkey and Italy.A few players came from Kaizer Chiefs, Mamelodi Sundowns and Orlando Pirates.Africa's most popular national team Nigeria, had just been pulled out of the matches due to political reasons.General Sani Abacha was in office and his coming into power, which was deemed by the United States and Europe as illegitimate, blatantly put,a coup-de-tat.The Super Eagles had just been robbed of an opportunity to defend the prestigious cup they had won in 1994 in Tunisia.This meant that Zambia, Egypt, Ghana and Cameroon were favourites to win the cup. By virtue of being hosts, South Africa was viewed as a potential winner according to pedestrian analysis.

Here in the 1996 Afcon, Doctor Khumalo's strongest weapon was simply his God given talent. The ability to do anything with the ball pleasing both his crowd and expressing himself. This confidence was necessary. What struck me the most about Doctor Khumalo was his complete synchronisation with the match around him.He was able to absorb all the information the game was in process of printing out. And his slow motion lope was massively deceptive because he consumed the manicured turf beneath his feet with ease.He would take a moment to run into spaces that others had vacated,then with that automatic 180 degree left-right twitch of the head,then reconnoitred the area,assimilating all data and saving information into his hard drive for later.When the ball got to him,his control was so instinctual that he rarely needed a second touch to position the ball for its next move. His first touch had done that for him already. That separated him from many South African players.With all the terrain and data stored, being processed,it was as if he was several passages of play ahead of anyone else. With intelligent team mates like Shoes Moshoeu, Phil Masinga or Mark Williams, danger was never far away. Doctor Khumalo was just top class. Top quality. I took a great deal of time to study midfielders. Thomas Madigage was phenomenally gifted. Zane Moosa was a magician. Ace Khuse was refreshingly intelligent. Roger Feutmba was arrogant on the ball,silky,creative and out of this world. Thabo Mngomeni was a genius, Junaid Hartley possessed unprecedented ability. Paul Gascoigne was the ultimate genius. Zinedine Zidane was Feutmba multiplied tenthfold. Pele Ayew was quite a beast. Paul Ince was a gritty,all-rounded talisman. Sebastian Veron was truly gifted, combative, creative but durable. Seydou Keita was enterprising, an unbelievable midfield schemer-in-chief, always negotiating life for his team. Shoes Moshoeu was industrious, authorative, brainy, powerful and above all, balanced. Ernest Chirwali was a compelling midfield creative. Jay Jay Okocha was another creative, a balanced genius. Rivaldo was unbelievable. Ronaldinho was a professor of football. Thabo Mooki was a master on the ball.Teko Modise was generally a commanding thinker but Doctor Khumalo, to me-was a preposterously gifted visionary, a generous creative who often scored important goals. His talent, was the true definition of beautiful football. He was truly out of this world.

When Shoes Moshoeu was in a devastating mood, Doctor Khumalo controlled the right midfield with imperious, almost arrogant authority. Doctor Khumalo was always aware of the non-stop runs made by the fast-paced Mark Williams at Bafana Bafana. He knew when and where to locate the late Phil Masinga. At Kaizer Chiefs, it would be Fani Madida doing those runs. Doctor Khumalo and Ace Khuse were Chiefs midfield architects who religiously and diligently dished sublime passes, long and short.

In the 1996 Afcon, Bafana Bafana started off well in Group A drubbing Oman Biyik's inspired Cameroon 3-0 at the 80 000 filled FNB stadium. Bafana went on to beat Angola 1-0 before succumbing to a narrow 1-0 defeat to Egypt. Bafana Bafana led the group with Egypt behind.

They would face favourites Ghana in the semi final. Former Olympique Marseille midfield magician Abedi Pele led the Ghanaians.He was already in the twilight of his career. Frank Amankwah was another talked about player running down the flank for the Ghanaian pride. There was the underrated Charles Akunnor in midfield. The Kuffour brothers were already star players in Europe and Africa.Osei Samuel Kaffour would later become a world-renowned super star starring for Bayern Munchen against Machester United in a hotly contested Champions League final. Leeds United's Lucas Radebe looked after the more dangerous Anthony Yeboah of Leeds United. Doctor Khumalo's roommate for the tournament John Shoes Moshoeu, was absolutely merciless when Bafana Bafana met Ghana.His enterprising performances saw the West Africans crash to a 3-0 defeat.Shoes Moshoeu noticeably had a good time that night.He was a talisman who could do no wrong. Shoes Moshoeu was unapologetically at his insulting best against the Black Stars. Doctor Khumalo, who had missed Bafana's group match against Egypt contributed significantly to this victory. What was more spectacular was his showboating which resulted in him getting a yellow card. Doctor Khumalo got himself booked for standing on the ball while the game was in play, which FIFA prohibits. Supporters liked it. That day, Doctor Khumalo just seemed hellbent on playing to the gallery. He knew that Ghana was dead and out. South Africans in the stands and the team on the field were prodigiously embued with euphoria. But the referee was not impressed. He flashed out a yellow card to South Africa's most popular soccer player, Doctor Khumalo! The yellow card was inconsequential as Bafana Bafana trooped on to the final.

South Africa would face strong North Africans Tunisia in the final.Tunisia had seen off the impressive Zambian team led by Kalusha Bwalya in the semi finals. A prolific Mehdi Ben Slimane at the forefront of their attack. Kalusha had been in a devastating form scoring impeccable goals in the group stages. It was interesting that the less fancied Tunisians would suddenly become a major talking point in the tournament. South Africa would have to be extra careful. It was Lucas Radebe who had the overwhelming task of taking care of the revered striker Ben Slimane. Ben Slimane was a fast paced, lethal finisher who had made a name for himself with his prolific prowess in front of goal. Seasoned Chokri El-Quar was at the time-by far the best goalkeeper in business at the time manned the posts for Tunisia. Clive Barker, together with his technical team consisting of Jomo Sono, Phil Setshedi, Peter Nyama and Budgie Byrne had to be strategic and shrewd in their planning. Doctor Khumalo had to be more involved than ever before. Doctor Khumalo would have to do some defensive work despite the presence of Victoria Setubal's Eric Tinkler in the field. Doctor Khumalo would also need to be a bit quicker when South Africa were in possesion of the ball to help the strike force get the ball as quickly as possible. It was a highly contested affair. Highly tactical. Intense stuff. World class.

In the second half, Mark Williams of Wolverhampton Wanderers came on as a substitute to recharge South Africa's strike force. Williams would instantly become a superstar. Williams scored in the 72nd minute, converting a chance by Eric Tinkler, later Mark Williams converted the second goal after being set up by a rather cheeky Doctor Khumalo pass. The tactically superior Tunisia collapsed. These goals catupulted Bafana Bafana into a historic African Nations Cup victory never envisaged by a fairly new democracy and the world at large. The result plunged the whole nation into a jamboree. It was a mayhem. The country turned into a carnival of excitement. This euphoria truly united South Africa.

Nelson Mandela had just got out of Robben Island 6 years ago. He was now State President of the Republic. President Mandela had also separated from his wife Winnie Mandela. Without a wife-and with his daughter, Zendzi not available to accompany him on this historic Afcon final, one Rochelle Mtirara came into the limelight. Rochelle, a supremely beautiful woman would regularly walk alongside the esteemed African statesman. Rochelle wore Bafana Bafana replica jersey number 15! This was Doctor Khumalo's popular jersey number. This prompted unprecedented curiosity across the country amongst the public. The media too, got curious and investigated.

It was understandable that Mandela wore replica jersey number 9 which was Captain Neil Tovey's famous jersey number. President Mandela would later rise to the podium with Captain Neil Tovey to lift the trophy. Interestingly though, attention somehow, somewhat immediately tilted towards a mysterious young woman who held hands with the world's most popular statesman. This lady,was wearing jersey number 15! Why 15? And who is she? The nation pondered….

It would later appear that Rochelle was a young Xhosa woman from the Thembu dynasty of the Mandela family. Rochelle was a young, vibrant and glamorous woman variously described as a grand daughter of President Mandela. Soon, Rochelle would obviously be linked to Doctor Khumalo in various public fora. Sunday papers sold well, alledging that the two were in a relationship! Neither Doctor Khumalo or Rochelle Mtirara would ever publicly state that indeed they were in a relationship or not. The media, like most of us soccer fans and supporters, could only speculate. My efforts too, in my curious attempts to establish the truth for this book, have been fruitless, in fact largely constrained.

It appears that the Rochelle Mtirara and Doctor Khumalo story was never really an issue to Doctor Khumalo. Afterall, Doctor Khumalo has always been linked to several beauty queens throughout his illustrious career. For the longest time, Doctor Khumalo was linked to the gorgeous celebrity radio and tv presenter Melanie Son. Briefly, he was linked to the beautiful and adventurous Pinky Masemola. There was also the R&B starlet Ntokozo Masinga in the picture. The media also linked him to the sultry Afro Pop star, the late Lebo Mathosa. These are some of the beauty queens that the media has linked to Doctor Khumalo over the years. So, the rumours about Rochelle Mtirara were never going to be such an issue to Doctor Khumalo. Various publications have always written that Doctor Khumalo's heart throb status brought him endless access to beauty queens. But the truth is that, this is absolutely normal. It is a universal trend that has engulfed many a superstar. Exceptional talent comes with all sorts of people and things. Both good and bad. All sorts of news. Good and bad. It would therefore, naturally come with the star status of Doctor Khumalo.

But the truth is that Nelson Mandela himself respected Doctor Khumalo as a sportsman. He probably also gave respect to Doctor Khumalo because Khumalo is a significant surname in the Zulu hierachy. The Mtungwa's are not ordinary people in the Zulu/Ndebele dynasty. History teaches us about the great Mzilikazi. Mandela himself was a Thembu Chief. Being a first class democrat he was, he however never abandoned his respect for culture, hierachy and traditional leadership.It appears that Mandela would probably not have minded or had any problem with the star courting his beautiful niece and grand daughter Rochelle. On the field, Doctor Khumalo was quite a astute player. He was extremely prudent as far as strategy was concerned. Doctor Khumalo on the pitch was manipulative, intelligent and incredibly flexible depending on the situation of play. He reminded me of the popular Chinese emperor Chairman Mao Ze Dong. Chairman Mao was a smart leader of the People's Republic of China in the 1950's. He directed operations of the Red Army with incredible skill, often beyond expectations of the enemy. The Red Army often advanced in great strides, puzzling and directing the nemesis, making them weary and finally succeeding in freeing itself from their pursuit. This was sheer brilliance. Chairman Mao was very sophisticated in operation that the enemy would never be able to understand his battalion. Doctor Khumalo just possessed that guile. He was so cryptic and unpredictable. So teams feard him. Supporters liked and adored him. The sponsors liked and respected him. He was the man. He still is the man today.

Doctor Khumalo was not different from Chairman Mao in manipulation. He would perform miracles with the ball. Doctor Khumalo often commanded the midfield with guile and pomposity. He dictated the flow of the match with precision in passing,incisive thinking and clinical finishing. He is known for changing the pace of the match, creating a rythmatic pattern with precise and discreet passes with Shoes Moshoeu. Shoes Moshoeu was in most cases, the partner in crime with his glittering and intelligent runs. Shoes Moshoeu was by far a supremely intelligent player. I watched Shoes Moshoeu carefully and closely during his heyday. He could have played for any club in the world. I also had the pleaure of interacting and chatting with Shoes Moshoeu on a few ocassions. Shoes was a human being and a half. The midfield also had steel strong Eric Tinkler. Sometimes it would be Linda Buthelezi or John Moeti who would do the dirty job. They chased back for the ball, throwing in the necessary tackles.Shoes Moshoeu had incredibly breathtaking speed, blessed with an amazing brain. He possessed both speed and balance. He was blessed with a vision of a hawk; a rare trait in South African football. He had quick one two's which left many opponents puzzled and in awe.Shoes Moshoeu would have complemented Benedict Vilakazi quite well had they played together.Vilakazi was another player who played intelligent, fast football. But Shoes Moshoeu was a truly amazing as a player. Fine and complete. Outside football, Shoes Msohoeu was a great personality. A truly humble legend despite his fame and fortune. He was a quiet but jovial individual you would mistake for a philosopher or an academic when you picked on his brain.

"I would like to think that in Shoes Moshoeu, we have a player who is among the best 10 players in the world,"Barker told Soccer News.

Clive Barker was summing the importance of Shoes Moshoeu in the team. Shoes Moshoeu was really head and shoulders above Bafana Bafana players at the 1996 Afcon in terms of performance.

Doctor Khumalo who was a relatively slow player himself, would cleverly position himself whenever the team regained possession-sometimes awaiting a pass from the inner part of his half.If and when he got the ball from his goalkeeper, Doctor Khumalo would make sure he unleashed a long defence splitting pass which in many occasions resulted in goal or at worst a corner kick.He was one of the best corner kick speacialists of his era.He kicked the ball with precision. He never just simply released the ball without first thinking. Bashin Mahlangu also had very good corner kicks. But Doctor Khumalo was more of an Andre Pirlo in terms of the way his corners were swung inside. Siphiwe Tshabalala is also a very good corner kick specialist. Teko Modise too. But Doctor Khumalo's corner kicks, more often than not, simply needed a striker to head into goal. The late Phil Masinga was the biggest beneficiary of these at Bafana Bafana.

Kalusha Bwalya, one of Doctor Khumalo's close football friends-was a talented left footed player who at the time showed flashes of brilliance which Doctor Khumalo also had. Kalusha is probably the most respected footballer in the Southern African region. He was born in 1963 in Zambia. Kalusha was voted African player of the year in 1988 and represented his country more than hundred times. He played in six African Nations Cups. Kalusha participated in the 1988 Olympics and scored a hatrick in the famous 4-0 victory over Italy in Spain.He played for FC Cercle Brugge Club in Belgium where he won two consecutive player of the year awards and top scorer respectively before moving to PSV Eindhoven. At PSV, Kalusha won the Championship in the 1990/1991 under Bobby Robson. Kalusha later went to play for Club America in Mexico where he later coached before retiring. He has been President of the Zambian Football Association and was also South Africa's 2010 World Cup Ambassodor. During the 1996 AFCON, Kalusha was influential in Zambia's third finish at the tournament winning the Golden boot. He was also a 1996 nominee of FIFA player of the year. Luckily, Kalusha was not in the ill-fated flight which killed the entire Zambian team in the Atlantic Ocean of Gabon in 1993.

Rochelle Mtirara was now busy celebrating in replica jersey number 15! Kalusha was wearing Doctor Khumalo's match jersey. Doctor Khumalo and Kalusha had exchanged jerseys despite the fact that Doctor Khumalo had just finished playing against Tunisia in a cup final! Kalusha had just played against Ghana whom where under the leadership of another equally gifted African superstar Abedi Pele Ayew.

Andre Pirlo was almost unknown when Doctor Khumalo did his magic. I wonder how and where Doctor Khumalo could have copied his dangerous corner kicks. Doctor Khumalo was also an adventurous penalty taker from his early days, feared by both opposition defenders and goalkeepers alike when in the box. When in possession of the ball in the box, I always knew that Doctor Khumalo would most likely force defenders to bring him down in his clever attempt to get a penalty. He converted most penalties with ease. Doctor Khumalo was simply an entertainer of some sort. He was seriously, honestly a beautiful football player. I usually only left the match immediately when Doctor Khumalo got substituted. Bad, but that's just how much Doctor Khumalo was influential to some of us growing up. The game looked parochial and poor without him. Sadly, I did the same whenever Siphiwe Tshabalala got substituted at Kaizer Chiefs because of the lack of creativity in their play which suddenly becomes apparent whenever Tshabalala is off the field.

It was during the end of Khumalo's career that he would miss a few penalties. It started off with a missed penalty in the 96 AFCON match against Algeria thanks to Mark Fish and Shoes Moshoeu who salvaged South Africa's pride both scoring in a narrow 2-1 victory. But this was uncharacteristic of Doctor Khumalo who for a long time in his career, was known as an enterprising corner and penalty kick specialist.

But the truth is that Doctor Khumalo was well known for his dribbling and intelligent passes more than anything else. He was also known for making defenders and goalkeepers look silly. He had extra ordinary ball skills. He would transform his dribbling into a profitable gesture when least expected. In 1998, he could not escape the wrath of one Paul Dolezar, a maverick Yugoslav-born French speaking coach. Dolezar was at the helm of Amakhosi during a derby match against traditional nemises Orlando Pirates.

Khumalo was in the opposition box, the ball fell onto his feet, and he dribbled a group of defenders. He looked over, saw a larger than life goalkeeper Williams Okpara in a dilemma, dummied him, with the net wide open, Doctor Khumalo hooked the ball up, lobbied it over the cross bar!The crowd went into silence! The stadium switched off. Nobody believed what they had just seen. Doctor Khumalo had made a spectacle out of the Pirates defence and goalkeeper, and missed because he wanted to score a spectacular goal. Pirates won the match 1-0.Doctor Khumalo had just commited the worst football mistake he had ever made on the football pitch. He had wanted to make Okpara and his defenders look silly.

"Don't ask me why we lost, ask Doctor, a professional," Dolezar said on TV immediately after the match. A "professional" as he said was clearly sarcasm veiled as disappointment. Dolezar was a Frenchman, very strict. He could however not say much more about Kaizer Chiefs favourite son. He had just made him lose a game that no coach wants to lose. Against Pirates!

Khumalo had just returned from the Major League Soccer in the United States.He had starred for Columbus Crew in Ohio. Prior to this, Khumalo had been labelled by detractors as an under achiever, given his preposterously immense talent. The expectation was that Doctor Khumalo should be playing in Europe already. Before all this, he had been on trial period with Aston Villa who because of work permit, could not sign him up. This was due to the difficulty that Europe faced when dealing with South Africa and its horrible policy of Apartheid. That policy killed many a dream, and buried many opportunities for black people of South Africa. However, others decried Doctor Khumalo's lack of speed as a problem that stalled his European dream.

"I have never been a fast player. Even when i started out, i was a slow player and i will remain that,"Khumalo defended himself.

A sympathetic section of the media and supporters cited his father's death as a causal nexus of a change in the star's game. Doctor Khumalo on his day was unbelievable. He played unbelievable football. He used his brains to outclass many opponents. In many a battle,

Doctor Khumalo came out unscathed. He often came out tops and triumphant. Doctor Khumalo just never really struggled with the ball.

Sun Tzu in the Art of War said "know your enemy and know yourself, in 100 battles you will never be defeated."

He further went to say "attack where the enemy is not guaranteed and catch him by suprise: defeat your enemy by a suprise!

Sun Tzu and The Art of war seem to have inspired Doctor Khumalo in the early 1990's. He planned intelligently and read his opponents' weakness in a diplomatic fashion. He would in most cases, suprise them with a suprise move, a *tsamaya*, a *shibobo* when something else was expected. Perhaps even when Kaizer Chiefs were trailing. That was Doctor Khumalo's strength. He played football to his own individual ability. That individual skill helped the team. It bonded them together. That ability saved Bafana Bafana and Kaizer Chiefs more often than not. It did not only save him, it also saved his legacy. It saved the legend and the brand.

Andy Moller, a great German player, Papi Khomane, Brendon Silent, Percy Molotsane, Elijah Litani and most recently Benedict Vilakazi in his farewell match, were some of the victims of Khumalo's famous and nasty *shibobos*. In his earliest days, defenders kicked him into pieces in a bid to silence and have him substituted before he could cause havoc with his mesmerizing skills. So Doctor Khumalo played wide out, in the flank, more like a luxury player. Swinging in those crosses, those long intelligent passes. However, many players became victims of his trickery nevertheless.

To many, Doctor Khumalo is simply the finest player to have come out of South Africa after the likes of Kaizer Motaung, Jomo Sono and Ace Ntsoelengoe. Whilst I am often tempted to believe what old generations say, about the trio being technically better than Khumalo, what strikes me is his popular appeal. It appears, at least to me, that his appeal to the masses is more widespread than that of the three legends. Yes, Jomo Sono is without a doubt an icon to many. He is without doubt the poster boy superstar of South Africa before democracy. My father always spoke highly of Jomo Sono. I could see the truth in his eyes whenever he spoke about Jomo Sono. Jomo Sono meant a great deal to the people his age. For black men working in the mines of South Africa during apartheid, Jomo Sono emanated and epitomized hope. In the same way that Mirriam Makeba brought hope to black women across South Africa and the continent. Jomo Sono was a symbol of freedom. He is the truest definition of black success. I have met the great Jomo Sono thrice, twice in Cape Town and once in Johannesburg. There is just this aura about him. But Jomo is just himself, original, quite good-humored but intensely enterprenueral in thinking and conversations. I have only seen his extra ordinary goals on television. Breathtaking! However, Jomo Sono is astonishingly very modest about his extraordinary success. Botsalo Ntuane, a prominent politician in Botswana always speaks highly of Jomo Sono, even publicly. He often equates Jomo Sono to Maradona! I am told that Kaizer Motaung was a prolific, left footed goalscorer, clinical in front of goal. He was adored by Pirates fans. The little I saw of Ace Ntsoelengoe was compelling. He was a clever and intelligent creative genius. Incredibly popular. However, for me Doctor Khumalo is completely different from many, and quite ahead in terms of mass appeal. Probably because I saw very little of Jomo Sono the player. Possibly because Jomo Sono belonged to many generations before me. Doctor Khumalo is palpably still the most loved soccer star today in South Africa. I must concede that Jomo Sono is said to have been a football King of the 70's and 80's. Extremely popular. Ok, Jomo Sono aside, since I started watching soccer around 1992, up to now, South Africa has not produced a player as famous as Doctor Khumalo. Walter Mokoena, a respected television and soccer personality in Africa describes Doctor Khumalo as "the most celebrated player of his generation, a real poster boy..." Lucas Radebe, Mark Fish, Benni McCarthy and Steven Pienaar are without doubt world renowned stars. They have played at the highest level. But they are surely still not more popular than Doctor Khumalo in South Africa. I don't quite know why this is so. Itumeleng Khune, Teko Modise and Siphiwe Tshabalala are extremely popular players today. But have they reached the level of Doctor Khumalo in terms of popularity? Teko Modise and Siphiwe Tshabalala are big, gifted players with big international brands behind them. But the truth is that they are both sadly in the twilight of their careers. Ok, besides great football skills, Modise is well known for his larger than life personality with a supreme appreciation of finer things in life. Exotic clothes and expensive sports cars. Tshabalala is well known for his commitment, flawless humility and impeccable sportsmanship. This also meant that the duo became symbols of big brands which pay them handsomely. But I can confidently say that they have both been a bit unfortunate in challenging for Doctor Khumalo's crown. Itumeleng Khune is quite close to Doctor Khumalo in terms of brand portfolio. Khune's acrobatic skills in goal posts have actually done him a great deal of favor in financial terms. Khune's widely publicized relationship with the super attractive TV personality Minnie Dlamini meant that the media focused on his life beyond the 90 minutes. Without doubt, the relationship really made them very, very popular. That relationship endeared the couple to millions of people who had keen interest in their life. The couple has since parted ways and Minnie Dlamini is now married. Like Doctor Khumalo, Khune is blessed with relatively good looks. But so are George Lebese, Ronwen Williams, Mpho Makola, Dean Mekoa, Kaizer Motaung Jr, Jimmy Tau and Mthokozisi Yende amongst others. But they have not had Doctor Khumalo's or Khune's exceptional media coverage and fame. But for Khune, this has really worked magic for him in terms of lucrative endorsement deals and popularity. I honestly still do not know exactly why Doctor Khumalo was that popular. It could very well mean that the advent of social media has really not helped the current stars as expected. Unlike in the years gone by, there is just so much activity out there. During the days of Doctor Khumalo and Mark Fish, the media focus was just on them. Today Khune shares fans and supporters with the likes of Floyd Mayweather. Some follow your Ronaldo, Neymar, Zlatan, Mbappe, Jay Z etc. Back then without Instagram and facebook, it was Doctor Khumalo or nothing. The newspapers focused on local stars. The English Premier League and the Spanish leagues were still there but not out there as we see them today. These leagues are so popular. They are like a religious edict now.That may be the explanation why there was so much attendance of local matches then than today. Brands marketed themselves fiercely through soccer stars like Doctor Khumalo. Today, there are many options. Rugby is now more fashionable amongst the black elite. Some black families watch and play cricket. Today you have the Brian Habana's and the Kagiso Rabada's of this world in sports codes not historically synonymous with black people. Television has also improved a great deal. There are many options today. Pay Television has also really changed the dynamics of sports and life in general.

Ok, let's go back to Doctor Khumalo's game. Pace could have probably been an issue for any coach. But Doctor used his brains to erase what could have been a significant problem in his game.When in possession of the ball, he was at his best.He would not let it go away from him easily-holding onto it until a team mate made an intelligent run, Mark Williams for example. This he did,on a number of occasions, like when he played at Chiefs when Amakhosi had an average 1995/1996 season. They had average players. Khumalo had a tendency of holding onto the ball. He would drive the ball half the pitch or he would make a team mate make an intelligent run by releasing a long accurate pass for the team mate to run on to it. Taking responsibility.

Doctor Khumalo is on record about his admiration for Roberto Baggio. For many years, he idolized the likes of Jomo Sono, Teenage Dladla, Ace Ntsoelengoe, Joel Mnini, Socrates, Pele, Johan Cryuff and Zinedine Zidane. It was no suprise that Doctor Khumalo had a little of most of these greats in him.As a young boy growing up in Soweto, he had watched a lot of De Stefano and Johan Cryuff on videos. His desire to become a much better player grew considerably. I have watched a few tapes of Ace Ntsoelengoe playing, although he possesed an incredible amount of skill, his major difference with Doctor Khumalo is that he was also extremely quick. Doctor Khumalo was generally slow.I must admit that it's a pity that i have only watched quite a few games that Ace Ntsoelengoe played. I was however immensely impressed by his talent. I agree that Apartheid irreversibly cost South Africa a place on the world stage of football. Junaid Hartley and Zane Moosa's abilities reminded me of the late Ace Ntsoelengoe who was quick but also very skillful.Clive Barker is a great admirer of Ace Ntsoelengoe. This is how he decribes the East Rand's finest soccer son.

"Ace Ntsoelengoe was interestingly skillful. He had trickery similar to that of the French master Zinedine Zidane. They both displayed the rare characteristics of being perfectly balanced, releasing the ball at the right time, never being hurried and able to read and dictate the game better than anybody else can in their respective eras in football," Barker said.

Clive Barker went on to say more about Zidane after Bafana Bafana played the French squad.

"I was fortunate to watch the sublime skill of Zidane of Real Madrid and my mind flashed back to the game when Bafana played France in the build up to the World Cup 98.We led 1-0 at half time, courtesy of a goal by Shaun Bartlett.France went on to win 2-1 in a hard fought match, the catalyst for this whole turnaround was Zidane.His magnificent presence on the football field is what impressed the most. He completely controlled the way his team performed in the 2nd half. For me, he is the Beethoven of football."

In the late 80s players such as Ace Ntsoelengoe, Scara Thindwa and Teenage Dladla were in the twilight of their careers. Doctor Khumalo was therefore used sparingly in the star studded Chiefs team which had the speedy and lethal Marks Maponyane, Ntsie Maphike and Wellington Manyathi. Doctor Khumalo positioned himself very well to take over from the great players Chiefs had.It was already obvious that Doctor Khumalo was going to be a gem.He had shown it against Orlando Pirates on his debut in 1987! He was a truly precise replacement of the genius Ace Ntsoelengoe. Recently in Klerksdorp, Sylvester City Kole told me it's unfair to compare players, especially Doctor Khumalo and Shoes Moshoeu, Jomo and Ace Ntsoelengoe.

"Doctor was a great player, Jomo Sono was exceptional but Ace was a genius. However, Shoes was all rounded, brilliant and balanced, more like Ace Ntsoelengoe. But you see, it's unfair to compare players. Each player has their own strengths," Kole said.

The arrival of the likes of Shane McGregor, Donald Khuse from Mamelodi Sundowns and Fani Madida saw yet another turn of events in 1992 when Amakhosi won almost unchallenged the league honours. McGregor and Madida were instant heroes in front of goals with the latter scoring a record that stood until one prolific Collins Mbesuma broke it in 2004/2005 season.

Khumalo was a major supplier of goals during Madida's hey days although mostly swung in as crosses as a winger. That position made him play close to the fans, under tremendous pressure. He had no choice but to deliver. He would have his name chanted all over the stands. When he recieved the ball, the crowd would stare, wait in anticipation for something special. He was just that amazing, unpredictable and predictable at the same time.

In this era, only a handful of the players could do it in local football. An immediate example is Junaid Hartley, an immeasurably talented Wits University product whose career suffered courtesy of many self-imposed set backs due to a poor disciplinary record off the field. Junaid briefly donned Orlando Pirates colours and played for several other clubs in the South African elite league such as Ajax Cape Town and Maritzburg United. He even had several spells overseas notably with RC Lens in France. Junaid played for Bafana Bafana five times while he represented all the national junior teams. Based on his enormous talent, this is not a good resume for Junaid Hartley. Junaid himself was a well known admirer of Doctor Khumalo. My view is that since the days of Doctor Khumalo, Junaid Hartley is one immediate player that came close to Khumalo in terms of skill and talent. The youngster could do almost anything with the ball on air or ground, it did not matter where. It is sad that Junaid retired from the beautiful game prematurely. Junaid Hartley has since gone public in varied publications about his previous off the field misdemenours which ended his once promising career. Junaid has been undergoing rehabilitation at home.

I honestly admired Junaid Hartley a great deal. I believed he could go all the way as a footballer. His advantage was that he was very quick. Doctor Khumalo was generally slow. Junaid Hartley was more like Jay Jay Okocha. Like Zane Moosa. Clever and just very quick. More like Ronaldinho. Doctor Khumalo was more like Zidane in play. He was not fast and relied more on skills and intelligence. But Doctor Khumalo was too smart and quite professional. He knew that he had that weakness but had enough respect for the game to play longer. Doctor Khumalo respected coaches and the job at hand. Tragically, Junaid Hartley has gone out publicly to blame the wrong crowds that surrounded him and the bad choices he made during his career. Doctor Khumalo had not only his father Eliakim, a legend in his own right but he also had the Motaung family who remain very close to him up to this day. Khumalo himself admits that Kaizer Motaung has known him since he was a toddler. Therefore Kaizer Motaung's eye has always been on Doctor Khumalo both on and off the field. Kaizer Motaung has always treated him as his own son. Doctor Khumalo went to school and played with both Kaizer's sons Bobby Motaung, who is the current Kaizer Chiefs Football Manager and the late Thabo Motaung.

Thapelo Liau is another player who had it all in him. A much travelled player who made headlines after signing a lucrative deal with Orlando Pirates only to play a handful of games before he was released. He was generally unlucky with coaches who also cited his lack of pace and application as his major undoing. However, Liau continued to play in the top league with other clubs despite limited game time. He later quit football and started a construction business. Liau was an enormous talent who took early retirement from soccer largely because of his pace despite his obvious talent.

Jabu Pule is another sad story. A player who could have gone to greater heights and played in any league in the world. He hypnotized Luis Chilavert's Paraguay at the 2002 World Cup. Jabu Pule played for South Africa from junior teams upto Bafana level. He had an overseas spell in Austria but could have probably played in the English and Spanish leagues had he listened to good advice. Jabu was a quick, extremely skillful player but generously shared the ball with his team mates. While Khumalo was not known for powerful shots, Jabu Pule could unpack a scotcher from any angle of the field to score a goal. He could dribble at an amazing pace. Pule used to do all the international stuff that Sir Alex Ferguson or Felipe Scolari would need from a player but at a speed never seen before in local football. In Jabu Pule, South Africa had Jomo Sono, Ace Ntsoelengoe and Doctor Khumalo, all in one package!

Jabu Pule is arguably South Africa's most famous player since Doctor Khumalo. He made his professional debut in a Telkom Charity cup tournament with a goal against Orlando Pirates. I watched Jabu Pule on many occasions, live. He was a phenomenon. He was enterprising with captivating performances week in, week out. He had crowds behind him, cheering him on. Jabu Pule terrorized a lot of teams and became an overnight superstar. As a Doctor Khumalo fan, Pule's rise to stardom baffled me. Shuffle, as was affectionately known was just too good. Fans loved him. He was a true heir to Doctor Khumalo's crown and throne. Unfortunately, as is the case with a lot of many young black people with lots of money, coming from poor backgrounds, Jabu Pule could not handle the fame, the money and everything that came with it. Muhsin Ertugrul had gotten him a club in Austria but Jabu Pule was sent back home to South Africa after a widely reported car accident. He came back to join Supersport United and later Orlando Pirates. Here, he just was not the Jabu Pule we knew from Amakhosi. Jabu Pule also tried to resuscitate his career at a 3rd division club in Sweden. It didn't work out. He returned home and was given a lifeline by Stan Matthews and Khulu Sibiya at Supersport United to play. The coach at the time Cavin Johnson helped him a great deal. Farouk Khan, a respected South African talent scout also helped Jabu Pule. Errol Dicks, the owner of FC Cape Town also tried to give Jabu Pule a salvation. It did not work out. Jabu Pule left the search for teams when Supersport presented him with an opportunity to work with the community. Jabu Pule grabbed it with both hands. He also got a job on their TV as a football pundit. Jabu Pule is now a reformed man doing film and motivational speaking. Jabu Pule's rags to riches story should be told as a matter of urgency, without apology. It is now more important for future generations.

Steve Lekoelea, Emmanuel Ngobese, Thando Mngomeni, Makalegs Siwahla and Shakes Ngwenya are just a few extra talented players who have shown flashes of brilliance that Doctor Khumalo exuded. However, most of them have been accused of lacking application and the much needed hunger. Some of them however, especially Shakes Ngwenya, was a victim of the lack of pace stereotype that is generally used. Shakes Ngwenya was no doubt one of the finest players South Africa has ever produced. He battled for a regular start at Sundowns and missed out on playing at the 2010 World Cup. He moved clubs including a stint in Vietnam. Shakes Ngwenya showed flashes of brilliance when he captivated fans in Botswana in the colours of Township Rollers. Ngwenya was discarded due to age and has since retreated back to township football where he seeks to develop talent.

Still at Township Rollers is Tshepo Matete affectionately known as Skhwama, a South African national signed from Baroka FC in the PSL. Skhwama is one of the most dangerously gifted stars to ever emerge from South Africa. A true township talent whose soccer strength is based on *tsamayas* and *shibobos*. When in form, Skhwama dribbled and showcased football skills I have never seen elsewhere at a pace Ronaldinho would simple marvel at. He drew Baroka FC lots and lots of supporters in their days in the National First Division. Even before that, he did the same playing township soccer in Limpopo and Soweto. Jagdish Shar of Township Rollers signed Skhwama probably to give his club more and more mileage and to draw large crowds to their matches. Like many of his talented peers of extra ordinary township talent, Skhwama did not play much in the highly competitive PSL. He was immediately seen as a surplus to requirements in the PSL. I see Skhwama as one of the biggest talents rejected by a system which is solely profit driven, with less interest in the thrill and the smile that such talent brought to the masses in the stands. I have not heard of any off the field shenanigans regarding Skhwama but the system rejected him without a fair chance. Sadly for Skhwama, most coaches think he is more of an entertainer than a footballer. At the time of publishing, Skhwama had been released by Rollers.

In one of his interviews, Khumalo once warned about the fame and fortune that more often than not disturbs the players' attitude and focus.

"When you ask me about these youngsters, I have to ask in response. Will they be able to take the criticism and pressure? The media will always be there to build you up, but they are just as quick to destroy you. If publicity goes to your head it will explode. These are the things I am scared of when I think of their future. I know because I loved the publicity. But publicity is the most dangerous thing for young players," Khumalo said.

The prediction that Doctor Khumalo feared almost became reality when the game lost a number of players such as Gift Leremi, Lesley Manyathela and a few others in unfathomable circumstances. The game also lost great players such as Skapie Malatsi, Sipho Nunens, Wayne Roberts,Junior Khanye, Lerato Chabangu amongst others to alcoholism and outrageous failure to handle fame and fortune. Their stories have been publicized in the media, with each one publicly giving great detail of how they lost focus.

Internationally, Jay Jay Okocha and Ronaldinho were well known dribblers but they were not similar to Doctor Khumalo.Doctor Khumalo is more similar to retired football master Zinedine Zidane.Zizou was slow but mastered dribbling. He just could not do without the ball. Interestingly, both Zidane and Okocha are some of Khumalo's favourite players.

"I think Doctor was a bit special than all our players because he had the natural skill, the guile and a penchant for great goals. I think had we discovered him earlier, and seen the right development,he would have been in the mould of Zinedine Zidane,"Ted Dimutru said in Kickoff.

Teboho Moloi is one of Doctor Khumalo's closest friends. Coincidentally, Moloi was a true replica of the famous Kaizer Chiefs legend in his play patterns. Moloi, although not very much a dribbler, the Pirates legend could do almost anything that Khumalo could do. He was a crafty and intelligent player. He would dictate Orlando Pirates midfield play in a similar way that fan favourite Teko Modise used to do at Pirates. Moloi always tried his best during matches to give Doctor Khumalo a tough time. Doctor Khumalo always emerged victorious because he scored goals particularly against Orlando Pirates. Moloi later went to play in Colombia and Turkey before coming home to Orlando Pirates for the last time in the late 90's before retiring at Bidvest Wits.He later came back to serve Orlando Pirates as an assistant coach. Moloi is still one of the most idolized players Orlando Pirates has ever had.

Moloi would admit that he never played much for Bafana because his 'replica' Khumalo-a better replica, was doing a good job for coach Clive Barker.Donald Ace Khuse was another player destined for greater heights playing in Turkey for a decade.He did well at Chiefs and represented Bafana Bafana a few times before having a misunderstanding with Barker.Khuse was an amazingly gifted player who could score goals.He could dribble and could pass the ball with unconceivable precision.His major undoing was that he passed the ball backwards more often than not. Ace Khuse remains one of the best players South Africa has ever seen having played for all the Big three, Sundowns, Kaizer Chiefs and Pirates. Ace Khuse is a highly esteemed individual, a near perfect professional and human being.

Thabo Mngomeni is another midfield virtuoso, a rare breed. Although not keen in displaying his skill, Mngomeni could play with the ball in the air with incomparable ease.Mngomeni went on to represent and captain South Africa.He was a workaholic, a dedicated and passionate player who happened to break into the limelight very late at the age of 28 years.He however brought the best out of his ordinary team mates at Umtata Bush Bucks. Rastaman, as was affectionately known, brought Pirates supporters to the games.His strength was that he was generous as a creative midfielder. He liked doing quick passes with another Pirates super star Benedict Vilakazi. Mngomeni was truly a great player who was clearly destined for greater heights. However, injuries cost him a career overseas and he quit the game after failed and protracted negotiations with Pirates supremo Irvin Khoza. Soccer fans still miss his extra ordinary goals. Mngomeni was involved in the 2010 World Cup soccer as Cape Town ambassador. He had earlier tried his hand at coaching at the now defunct Ikapa Sporting club.

Besides Doctor Khumalo, there were only two delicate official passers of the ball. It was always the late Isaac Shakes Kungoane and Cameroonian midfield genius Roger Feutmba.The latter was largely respected mostly because he would not do anything much but cheekly pass the ball to the next player. Perfectly. Doctor Khumalo had very stimulating moments against Roger Feutmba. They really competed well, with passes and great goals. Big brains. Feutmba had unbelievable skill. He had a large educated left foot with impeccable precision in passing. He was a true challenger to the throne. Feutmba was a midfield god in the league. Many people still do not understand what cut short Feutmba's career at Sundowns.The former fan favourite is now back home in Yaounde trying to cut a niche in coaching. He was a complete footballer in the true meaning of the word. Today, there is still some debate going as to who really is the finest foreign midfielder to have ever played in South Africa. It appears though, that the debate centres between Ernest Chirwali and Roger Feutmba. Understandably so.

Kungoane was a fan-favourite at Chiefs. He truly made football look easy,very easy. He was intelligent, played intelligent passes, long and short, with arrogance and flamboyance never seen in the local game. Shakes truly gave fans their money's worth. He played rib-tickling football. People loved his way of playing. Only coaches were against it. His penalty taking was beyond comprehension. He was a genius, an ultra gifted midfielder who contributed significantly at Amakhosi. Weight issues and lack of pace were obvious obstacles in his career. Coach Gordon Igesund would regularly argue that he benefited a great deal from Shakes passing while at Manning Rangers who won league honours in 1996/1997 season. Strikers George Komantarakis and Simon Makhubela were major benefectors in the team which was full of dedicated players like Clinton Larsen who won the league. The duo scored a lot of goals due to the generosity of Shakes Kungoane. Kungoane died a few ago after a cardiac arrest. Soccer fans still miss the smile he wore throughout the game. At the time of his death, Kungoane worked as a football analyst on TV.His football pudintry was full of humor, and so was his game and passing. This included his humor in taking spectacular penalties which the crowds appreciated more. He was a fantastic personality indeed as shown by the sorrow that sat on the faces of the multitudes who had come to bury him.

Sundowns' Zane Moosa was another massive talent. He was too fast. Nobody could read his game unless you really understood him. Sometimes he would even dribble his own team mates! He was just too sophisticated. He was a Ronaldinho type of dribbler. He would do many things with or on the ball within seconds. He was extremely fast and sometimes even fans would not see what he'd just done on an opponent. He was a marvel to watch and had a decent career that took him to Greece. Zane Moosa came back to briefly play for Kaizer Chiefs before religious commitments took him into early retirement. Besides Moneeb Josephs, Zane Moosa is one of the few Muslim players who have realy made a big name in the local game.

But truth be told, at the 1996 Nations Cup, all Bafana players who took part in the month-long spectacle were truly gifted. They were a fantastic bunch. I salute each and every one of them in this book. They brought hope to this nation. They are great patriots. However, there are some players that were not given special mention like Andre Arendse. Andre was born on the same month and year with Khumalo in 1967. He was not a fancy goalkeeper but was hugely talented. Above that,he was a true leader and a great professional. Arendse was born in Cape Town and started off his professional career with Cape Town Spurs where he won a league medal. He later had a brief spell with Oxford and Fulham in the United Kingdom before returning to win another league medal with unfashionable Engen Santos.He later achieved the same feats with both Sundowns and with Supersport United. Andre at 41 years old, was still going strong in the elite league. He is currently a goalkeeper coach at Bidvest Wits. Below is how Clive Barker described Arendse.

"His performances for Bafana Bafana are well documented and i endorse my previous comments on TV, and in the press that he's one of the finest sportsmen that i have had the privellege to know and work with," Barker said.

Andre was a lanky, tall, fearless, and athletic goalkeeper extremely committed to his game. He justifiably gained a reputation as one of the best in Africa at the time. He was a leading figure who wrestled his position from Steve Crowley, another talented goalkeeper who retired early.

Eric Tinkler of Victoria Setubal left Wits University as a young boy in 1987 and secured himself a future in Europe mostly in Portugal.Tinkler was not a particularly fancy player, but he was a very important player who worked tirelessly throughout. He won most of the balls and packed a fierce shot. He kept the hugely talented but hard-tackling Linda Buthelezi on the bench on many occasions. Tinkler came back after two decades in Europe and was developed by his former club Bidvest Wits as a coach before he joined Orlando Pirates. He later joined Cape Town City where he was hugely successful as head coach in his first year. The achievement landed Tinkler the more lucrative job of Head Coach at the wealthy Supersport United although for a very short spell.

Another player who made South Africa tick was Neil Tovey.He was a no-nonsense player as well. He was more like Tinkler. The nice thing about Tovey is that, like red wine-he was very mature and disciplined. He was never going to be useless. He was a good organizer, a true leader who communicated very well with his goalkeeper.Tovey was a clever player who was always in check. He was relatively tall but not a physically gifted player like Morgan Gould.He respected the game and was also respected by the football industry as a whole. Tovey is now involved with SAFA as a Techinical Director. Mokoko, as Tovey was affectionately known, is widely believed to be the best captain Bafana Bafana has ever had to date.

Tovey acknowledges in one of the defunct magazines Football Arena that Doctor Khumalo has been a real inspiration to many people in South Africa.

"Doctor is a huge symbol of success to young boys and most of them aspire to be like him. He was by far the most recognizable figure in the Bafana team,"Tovey said.

(6)

France 98, World Cup

Rarely has a national side entered a world cup as such strong favourites as Brazil did at France 98.To find pararells,one has to look back perhaps as far as Ferenc Puskas in Swirtzerland in 1954.Whereas the Hungarians had been unbeaten in three years and tipped the footballing world upside down by humiliating England 6-3 at Wembly 1953,and then for good measure stuffing them again 7-1 in Budapest just a few months later, Brazil could not lay claim to anywhere near such form.That Hungary team would ultimately lose the final in 1954 to West Germany 3-2 having been 2-0 up after just 8

minutes and cruising, remains one of football's greatest conundrums. Even more when you consider that the Hungarians had routinely buried the Germans 8-3 in a group game less than two weeks earlier. There would be similarities in Brazil's campaign in France.When Brasil arrived at France 98, their billing as favourites was somewhat contrived and based largely on two things namely;

1.Ronaldo and the lack of viable alternatives. Ronaldo was obvioulsy the best footballer in the world at the time. With two consecutive Fifa World Player of the Year gongs, he had easily wooed the world's coaches and brought back to the game some of the colour not seen since Brazil side of 1970.

2, at France 1998, there were no real stand out teams who demanded attention. There were the usual suspects-however of coarse, such as Italy, Holland, Germany, but although each were good, none was really outstanding. The French had looked ill equiped to take advantage of their hosting advantage. In fact, in all fairness, no one gave them a realistic chance especially having failed to qualify for USA 1994.The situation that South Africa found themselves in, having failed to qualify for Angola 2010 Afcon-Bafana Bafana were, in some quarters naturally expected to win the 2010 World Cup that they would host. But in football, nothing is predictable. In the local parlance, commonly popularized by the late larger-than-life football commentator Cebo Manyaapelo; "football has no therefore" essentially meaning that the beautiful game is inherently unpredictable.

Another factor which was also prevalent in catapulting Brazil to the forefront of everybody's thinking was Nike. By now Nike, leviathan football marketing machine was in full swing and what an impressive beast it was.With Ronaldo, the best player in the world at the helm and his seemingly dependable ability to win games single handedly,it was Nike more than the world's press who had made Brazil the hot favourites of the tournament.They spent a fortune on two campaigns in particular.One being the ad where giant billboards which featured Nike around the world reflecting the global nature of the world cup.But the real winner which few will never forget is the TV advert that Nike released ahead of and during the finals which sold an impression that Brazil was an unbeatable dream team. This was extra ordinary. The sponsorship power translated into the player confidence. It was a marvel to watch for most of us. This was extra ordinarily interesting. Intrigue and Pressure.

Kappa, long time Bafana technical partners had not done this with South Africa and so there was no pressure on the boys. Doctor Khumalo had no new advert and PUMA-his personal sponsors for many years now, even today in retirement had not come up with any intimidating spectacle as an advert. But the whole hyper commercialisation of the Brazil team was understandable. They had in their team not only Ronaldo but Roberto Carlos, Cafu, Denilson, Edmundo, Caesor Sampaio, Rivaldo, Dunga, Ze Carlos and Emerson amongst others. Mario Zagallo was at the helm of this galaxy of stars. South Africa was in a relatively tough group considering the French team and their host status. The Danish team was full of spirited players such as the Laudrap brothers. There was basically very little or nothing to talk about in respect of the Saudi Arabia team.

Nelson Mandela, just like any other hosting President was hopeful and expectant.He met regularly with the boys to give them a word of encouragement.He had been impressed by the spirit of the 1996 AFCON victory.

"The debate will continue in South Africa about who was the greatest footballer our country has ever produced. I'm convinced that your name will always feature among the candidates … this world cup affords you the opportunity to settle this debate once and for all," Nelson Mandela said this to Doctor Khumalo.

This was South Africa's maiden appearance at the world's greatest soccer show.Bafana Bafana had just come out of a hard fought battle to win their group.South Africa had never gotten an opportunity to compete internationally with other nations due to the sanctions placed on it because of its racist policies implemented by the racist National Party government.

In France, they would play against the hosts France, Denmark and Saudi Arabia.Back home in South Africa, people were embued with the spirit of patriotism and euphoria, well behind Bafana Bafana and the technical staff under the guidance of Philippe Troussier.In fact immediately after the Congo match which qualfied South Africa for France 98, a police spokesperson Andy Pieke told AFP that over 300 people got injured in post match violence and were hospitalised.

"There's an unusual number of casualities in hospitals. The number has exceeded 300 and this is not only at FNB stadium but across Johanessburg," Pieke said.

This meant that the expectations of supporters and the nation had been reasonably raised by the spirited performance of the boys against a stuborn Congolese team.

Philippe Troussier was born in France in 1955. He had coached a number of national teams like Burkina Faso, Nigeria and popular clubs such as Asec Abijan.Philippe was first brought to South Africa by Chiefs supremo Kaizer Motaung.

Philippe was a disciplinarian who espoused a strict regime complimented by an uncomprising attitude. He had assembled a youthful team perhaps with exception of Lucas Radebe, Doctor Khumalo, the late Shoes Moshoeu, the late Phil Masinga and Brendon Augustine. Augustine was a hard working striker who played for Bush Bucks in South Africa before going to play for Austria's Lask Linz.He had just had a bad season at club level.Augustine would later be dismissed from camp in France for disciplinary reasons together with Naughty Mokoena. New blood included Spanish based Quintone Fortune, Benni McCarthy,Pierra Issa,Hans Vonk and Alfred Phiri.Issa is a Germiston-born player of Lebanese descent who migrated to France at the age of four.He was called to the squad most probably for his aerial ability. It is very possible that he was also called in because of his command of the French language since Troussier was a Frenchman. The 1998 World Cup was played in France. Left-footed Maimane Alfred Phiri was a 24 year old, very promising youngster who had only played a few matches in South Africa before getting a lucrative move to Vanspor in Turkey.Phiri was a workaholic of note. Off the field, he was a team player with an amazing personality.Phiri had made his debut against Zambia a month prior to the World Cup but was seen as a suprise inclusion.He mastered deceptive set pieces and was useful with both feet.He would spend almost a decade in Turkey before returning to the PSL where he made a name at Moroka Swallows and Ajax Cape Town scoring spectacular goals in the process.Phiri, unlike Pierre Issa is now a legend and role model to millions of South African youngsters.He organises the most succesful off season tournament in the Townships of South Africa.A great number of players in the professional ranks were discovered there.Phiri played until he was in his late 30s. While at Ajax

Cape Town, I bumped into Phiri a few times. A football man through and through. Phiri is a down to earth individual who has not been changed a bit by fame and fortune. Phiri acts as an agent for Lebogang Manyama, a fast-paced Bafana Bafana winger.

Vonk was also an unknown. He had lived all his life in The Netherlands playing there. Vonk, who was born in Alberton in South Africa was plying his trade for SC Hereeveren in Holland. A lot of people wondered who he was. Vonk went on to prove himself in over 40 matches for Bafana as one of the best goalkeepers in Bafana Bafana history. He later joined Ajax Amsterdam afterwhich he joined their satellite club Ajax Cape Town where he retired after two great seasons. Vonk is currently Head of Football at Ajax Cape Town.

Khumalo had played a crucial role in qualifying Bafana Bafana for the prestigious soccer spectacle. But on their way to France, Bafana Bafana played a few friendly games against a select team in Germany and Iceland.I watched the matches on television at very odd hours. Khumalo did well in these matches. South Africa remained hopeful that Khumalo would form part of the starting eleven in the world cup. That has always been a given afterall.No one ever thought of Bafana Bafana eleven without Doctor Khumalo.The vision,the passes, the intellect on the ball and everything Khumalo had always been known for in local soccer would be expected of him to unleash against opponents at the World Cup. In Doctor Khumalo, South Africa had a playmaker of genius proportions. He was able to cast a spell over the ball. The most important question was; would Philippe Troussier be interested in the talent of the superstar?

Hard tackling Linda Buthelezi who was a very good passer of the ball would be robbed off the tournament by an injury and so was the late Phil Masinga who had scored South Africa's most famous goal that took the squad to the most prestigious tournament the World Cup.

19 year old Benedict McCarthy,a phenomenally gifted Cape Town-born striker,having emerged as joint leading goal scorer in the 1998 Afcon in Burkina Faso was the obvious choice upfront. He had also been voted Player of the Tournament in Burkina Fason.Masinga and Bartlett should benefit from Doctor Khumalo's intelligent pin point passses to advance South Alfrica to the second round at the least. Troussier had other plans. However, it all started with camp dividing into two. Apparently, some players complained about the coach's strict attitude against them while some approved his no-nonsense attitude. Trott Moloto, who was assistant coach at the time,was caught in a predicament. Captain Lucas Radebe, Shoes, Fish, Phil Masinga and Doctor Khumalo would hold meetings to help calm down the growing tension in the Bafana Bafana camp.

South Africa's opener was in Marseille. Against the star-studded French team,it was a total disaster. A young, fresh, super fast Thiery Henry ran down the defence of Radebe, William Jackson and Mark Fish throughout the match tearing the defence apart. Bafana lost 3-0! They were simply pathetic. There was no hope really. Pierre Issa, a French speaking South African of Lebanesse descent roped in to help in defence looked quite unsettled and destabilized. He made blunders, school boy errors and confused goalkeeper Hans Vonk.Issa suddenly got ostracized in the media back home in South Africa. Remember that the region also looked to South Africa as world cup representatives. To supporters who had pinned their hopes on Bafana, Issa had simply given the match to the French team on a silver platter. Issa later went on to play for Watford in England. He was one of the highly paid players in Watford history, signed by Gianlucca Vialli from Olympique Marseille. Issa proved to be an expensive flop at Watford and was put on transfer in February 2002. He later went back to Lebanon and later played in Greece.He represented South Africa 47 times but is still not fans favourite despite that amount of loyalty to his country. I must say that expectations at Bafana Bafana are wild and it often takes long for a player to register his name in the hearts of the people. A simple example is Bongani Khumalo; a big defender,one of the most successful players in the country having won the league on several occasions with Supersport United and now with Bidvest

Wits. Bongani was one of the unlucky players when he played for Bafana Bafana. It would appear that Bongani, even after signing a big money contract with Tottenham Hotspurs in the EPL,Bafana fans still continued to doubt his ability. Bongani is that player who always gave his best even when he made a genuine mistake. Bongani became more unpopular when he became captain of his club and subsequently Bafana Bafana and made more media appearances. His position of captain exposed him to periodic TV interviews where he spoke very good English with a fast and thick European accent. People generally felt that Bongani did not belong. He was born in Swaziland to an elitist black South African family who took him to the so-called Model C schools in Pretoria. People seemed to think that coaches made him favors because of his previlleged background. I have failed to establish whether Bongani Khumalo and Doctor Khumalo are related. It was the same with Kaizer Motaung Jr. Motaung Jr was a hugely lethal striker who was always fully committed to Kaizer Chiefs. To be fair to him, supporters never gave Motaung Jr a fair chance probably because of his european upbringing. Motaung Jr had gone through all the necessary developmental processes at Bidvest Wits. He did his A-levels at the highly prestigious Harrow School in England, where he would end up playing at Chelsea Reserves. He later moved to Germany where he linked up with 1860 Munich. Back home in South Africa, when Motaung Jr finally came back to sign for Kaizer Chiefs, people raised eyebrows. He would finish second top goalscorer with 12 goals behind Chris Katongo's 15 goals in the 2006/2007 season and people still ignored that feat. Motaung Jr was never the fans' favorite. Another prejudice is that many people simply held a preposterous thought that Motaung Jr simply played because he was the chairman's son. The other thing that really probably made people judge Motaung Jr was his versatility and history with cricket. He had represented South Africa at junior level in cricket. And supporters knew this. They subsequently simply chose not to see him as a soccer player. I also guess his good looks and affluent English accent generally seemed to make things worse for him. People, it would appear,generally had issues with his privileged background. Motaung Jr retired early from playing football to complete his University education. He is now fast emerging as an executive within the Kaizer Chiefs empire. Motaung Jr remains one of the fastest players i have ever watched in South African football. A shrewd striker who scored beautiful goals mostly with a header. Back to Issa, truth told, Issa was a very good player who was simply not liked by supporters for reasons that will possibly never be known. I truly believed in Issa as a defender as much as I believed in Motaung Jr's finishing ability. I also believed so much in Bongani Khumalo because he was not only a committed player but has all the physical attributes of an international defender. I do not believe that these players reached the level they reached in football by fluke. They were simply misconstrued. They were adversely judged on factors unrelated to their game.

In the opening match in France 98, Doctor Khumalo did not get a run in the match and thousands of South Africans were really upset at home. This was South Africa's first match at the highest, very top level of football. People, especially in the townships of Soweto and elsewhere in Botswana, Swaziland and Lesotho felt that Khumalo should have started the match ahead of the hard running but unknown left footed Alfred Phiri.Phiri had been overseas for long and was not well known in South Africa at the time. It appeared that people were fiercely against his inclusion ahead of Doctor Khumalo. Phiri made a massive blunder in that match, getting a red card that would also put more pressure on the already battling, nervous and under pressure Bafana Bafana. The red card would end Maimane Phiri's further participation at the world cup as he missed both matches against Denmark and Saudi Arabia respectfully.

France had Fabian Barthez who combined goalkeeper's eccentricity and flair in equal measure. He had a telepathic understanding with Laurent Blanc, as their ritual head kissing would be a common feature throughout the spectacle.Towering and intimidating Ghanaian-born fullback Marcel Desailly was there. There was Didier Deschamps who marshalled midfield with chutzpah and unflinching commitment. Enterprising Emmanuel Petit, fast-paced Thiery Henry, intelligent Christian Karembou, no-nonsense defender Frank Lebouf, the deadly Christophe Duggary, the tricky Stephane Guivarch, the larger than-life defender Lilian

Thuram and the master phenomenon Zinedine Zidane made the popular French team. This line up could have probably unsettled any team that was making its maiden appearance at that level. However, South Africans are a hopeful and resilient nation. They truly believe in their own resolve. That was evident when the leadership of the opposition ANC and PAC were on Robben Island and some in exile. The masses in the streets and the townships desperately hoped for the best. They believed that freedom would come one day. It did come. Eventually. For the world cup, fans and patriots simply respected that the man at the helm was Coach Philippe Troussier. They believed Philippe Troussier would take them to the Promised Land just like Mandela had done when he fought against white supremacy for nearly three decades on Robben Island. And after prison when he delivered democracy yearned by all, both black and white.

The hope was for a better much improved performance in the next match. But unfortunately, the opponent would be Denmark in Toulosse, with the likes of Peter Schemiechel. Peter was a great goalkeeper, at the time-the best in the world. The Danish keeper is probably by far, the best that Manchester United has had in history. Against the Scandanavians, Schemeichel's future teammate at Man United, Quinton Fortune who was with Atletico Madrid at the time, was another new comer to the Bafana fold. Quinton Fortune had a great day. He played with his heart out. He ran non-stop, with Shoes Moshoeu complimenting the youngster. The Danes were resolute until McCarthy blasted the ball through Peter's legs to give Bafana an equaliser. Fortune again fired a scotcher from a set piece that raised everybody's emotions. To the Danes that could have dampened their spirits in Coppenhagen and to South Africans in Johannesburg and elsewhere. Peter had a slight touch to the ball that hit the cross bar to deny Quinton Fortune. Khumalo was watching from the bench when the referee blew his whistle for full time. South Africa had one match left against the rich but less fancied Saudi Arabia. That, if he is not picked-would be the end of Khumalo's illustrious national team career. He was 31 years old with a remote possibilty that he would play in the next World Cup in 2002. He would be 35 years old then. But would South Africa even qualify for the 2002 World

Cup? A lot of players were itching for game time. Saudi Arabia would be their solace. This match,would be a life time opportunity of representing their country at the highest level, the world cup.

In SABC studios, Clive Barker had been called to do match analysis. He was spot on! He complained about Khumalo's exclusion. His point was that Doctor Khumalo could have given South Africa some form of shape in midfield. He would have hung onto the ball a bit longer and made the team not to play the european type of game because they were playing europeans: European teams needed a different approach because they are regular participants at this tournament, Barker opined.

In the last match, South Africa had to win this encounter against the Arabs in Boardeax's Par Lescure stadium. Doctor Khumalo was once again on the bench! He would only come on with 23 minutes remaining of the match in place of Fortune.He went in with Jerry Sikhosana, a slippery and lethal striker from Orlando Pirates who had become extremely famous in South African football. He had become famous for scoring important goals for Pirates against a talented Brian Baloyi of Kaizer Chiefs. Baloyi was South Africa's best known locally based goalkeeper, very talented and very popular. Before Jabu Pule, Baloyi was probably South Africa's most recognizable player after Doctor Khumalo.

People felt that Doctor Khumalo and Jerry Sikhosana had not been given a fair chance. Troussier was surely getting the complaints from home and introduced the duo. The performance against Denmark was a much-improved act. Khumalo exchanged a few clever passes with Sikhosana but the Arabs were not compromising. The damage had already been done and the match ended 2-2. FIFA gives the team that gets knocked out of the World Cup 24 hours to leave the host country. It would be a long long journey back to Africa.Troussier apparently never returned to South Africa. He was already home, in France. His home country. He then briefly coached Morocco but was fired after a difference of opinion. He converted to Islam in the Moroccan capital in 2006. He would now go on to coach Qatar, Olympic Marseille and Japan at the 2002 Korea/Japan world cup. He, in fact won the Asian Cup with the Japanese national team. His reasons for such a pathetic display with South Africa at the 1998 World Cup was that "I did not have a bench."

Millions of supporters, myself included-had to accept the reality that South Africa had just been sent home. Doctor Khumalo, by far the most talented player of his generation, the most celebrated soccer player in the country only had a cameo appearance at the World Cup! And against minnows Saudi Arabia! To many people, this was a traversty. Philippe Troussier boasts one of the more impressive international resumes having led three separate nations at three different world cups. He surely is not a mediocre mentor, pundits say. I still don't understand Philippe Troussier to this day. To be fair to the man,i should simply reserve my comment.

Nelson Mandela himself must have been a bit disappointed with the team's performance. Mandela had pinned his hope on the nation's cup hero Doctor Khumalo in particular, to make the world know that South Africa was a unified nation, not just politically but also in sport through victory.

Trott Moloto had to pick up the pieces after Troussier's resignation. Moloto had to bring back their confidence and belief. Trott had been assistant coach at Chiefs under Troussier in 1994. They both won the 1994 BP top 8 Final which i watched when they defeated Sundowns 3-2. Khumalo was one of Troussier's key players then-that made people sure that Doctor Khumalo would never struggle for game time at the national team under the French man.He never doubted 16v's talent nor did he ever suggest that Doctor Khumalo had passed his sell by date. A lot of things transpired in France during the world cup. It would appear that some players just never liked Philippe Troussier. His training methods were deep and quite strict. Troussier apparently preferred overseas based players particularly those who played in Europe because of a unique dynamic they brought to the squad.

One section of the media felt that Lucas Radebe was not ready to lead the team and that the tough tackling Leeds defender was just too soft as a leader. Lucas was a remarkably gifted defender who played over a decade for Leeds United in the English Premiership. During his time at Elland Road, Lucas won accolades from all quarters of the world for his dedication, discipline and commitment. He had played with Doctor Khumalo at Chiefs. In fact, Lucas in his own book, MADIBA" S BOYS writes that he was inspired by amongst others Doctor Khumalo when he got into professional football from Bophuthatswana. Lucas Radebe would then go on to greater heights and represented Bafana Bafana over 70 times, captaining the team in 44 matches. Lucas was on top of his career in 1998. He was a regular in England and captained Leeds for over six years of the eleven years he spent with the club. The Chief as he is often affectionately called, was respected by his opponents at the world cup. However, Lucas Radebe is said to be a generally sweet person who hardly complained. He would simply give you that Colgate smile even in the midst of adversity. He would find himself in a dilemma with a deeply divided squad in France.His strength, perhaps his weakness-is that he hardly bothered himself with off the pitch incidents. Radebe preferred to lead by example on the pitch. He was often criticized by some quarters of the media but he rose above this storm and held his head up. On international standards, Lucas Radebe and Benni MCcarthy are by far the most successful South African exports to date. Today Lucas is now a businessman with very prudent investments notably in the publishing industry. Lucas Radebe is also a highly sought-after motivational speaker. He does coaching clinics and is paid a fortune by big corporations who also want to associate with his brand. He was also a 2010 World Cup ambassador. Lucas Radebe was also awarded an Honorory Masters Degree by the celebrated University of Cape Town in 2005. Leeds Metropolitan University in the United Kingdom later conferred on him an Honorary Doctorate in Sports Science.FIFA would also bestow on him the prestigious FIFA Fair Play award. Radebe is a global football statesman.

However, some people in the media felt that Shoes Moshoeu or Mark Fish should have been made successor to Neil Tovey.Moshoeu was a naturally quiet person. An intelligent guy who rather preferred to be in his own space reading books. Like Radebe, Shoes shied away from the spotlight. Like Lucas Radebe, he preferred to lead by example on the field. Fish was a no-nonsense white player. He was well known for his good performances, particularly his long runs down the flanks. A physically gifted defender who also scored important goals. He broke into Bafana Bafana very early as a youngster from Orlando Pirates having been produced by Jomo Cosmos. His main undoing was that he could tell a club boss or SAFA official where to get off. Another player who was mentioned in this category of leaders was David Nyathi, a soft spoken but devastating left back who also preferred to do the talking on the field. Nyathi was highly respected by teammates and the media. He played in Spain and also played his heart out for his country. Nyathi like Shoes Moshoeu, spent most of his time minding his own business. At the time, Nyathi was playing for St Gallen in Switzerland. He came back to play for Kaizer Chiefs before retiring to Cape Town with his affable wife. I have interacted with Nyathi and his good wife as they reminisced to me about their good life back in Swirtzerland. A humble guy indeed. However, one school of thought felt that Philippe Troussier was simply not good enough. That he was really just a bad choice. Another school of thought held a view that the changes he made to the team that Barker had were drastic, suicidal and badly calculated. Rather quite unnecessary. This school of thought felt that SAFA should not have parted ways with Cliver Barker on the eve of the world cup. They argue that Barker should have been the man to lead South Africa at that France 1998 world cup.

SAFA was also in a quagmire. They were getting a lot of stick in both electronic and print media regarding Barker's resignation. The players themselves looked rattled and the morale was visibly low. That was palpable even in their play, prior to the 1998 World Cup during the friendly matches in Europe.

"Half of the team did not know whether they were coming or going. I did not want to cause ugly scenes but i had to play a part to help the guys get into the game. When i was put on against Saudi Arabia, it was as if the coach was saying; just go there and do whatever, by then the guys had already set their minds on returning home,"Doctor Khumalo told Kickoff.

Playing for Bafana Bafana changed since France 98. To many, it is no longer seen as a lifetime opportunity. Anyone can play for the team today. Relatively average players such as McDonald Mukansi, Siyabonga Sephika, Saul Molapo and hundred others went on to don national colours. In fact, Lebogang Morula-an unknown Vanspor midfield player, formerly at Jomo Cosmos also made the squad for the World Cup in France.But it could also be that South Africa went to France 98 with a polarised team.

Under Barker, it was tough for players to break through into the squad.Excellent players like Eric Ramasike, Thomas Madigage, Teboho Moloi, Ace Khuse, Fani Madida and numerous others did not get as many call ups as they should have got.Some would be called for several matches but would not be given a chance easily. These include the likes of Zane Moosa, Roger de Sa and Daniel Mudau. For example, Zane Moosa competed with a rare breed in midfield while Roger de Sa faced strong competition from Steve Crowley, Brian Baloyi and Andre Arendse. Daniel Modau was also unfortunate. He failed to displace the likes of Phil Masinga, Shaun Bartlett and Mark Williams up front. It was the selection of players who had come in that probably irked the likes of Doctor Khumalo.

"What was hurting...i do not know about the other guys, was that we had worked very hard to get the team to France and at the end it was a mess. People who contributed nothing were there but for what? Every South African supported the team in France and it took people who did nothing for the country to destroy the feeling. Upto today the spirit is not the same," Khumalo said.

This was relatively a feeling of many people not only in South Africa but the Southern African region as a whole was fully behind South Africa as the first in the region to participate at the world cup. The feeling was that because Barker had been fired under discreet, somewhat shady circumstances that the public felt was water under the bridge.

The other fact was that South Africa never really had good preparatory games as they played against minnows such as the VFB Stuttgart Reserves whom they walloped 5-0, Stuttgart Kickers whom they drew 1-1 with,Iceland and a 2-0 loss to Argentina,the 1-1 draw against Zambia.The only competitive matches they had were the famously thrilling 3-2 loss to a Bebeto inspired Brasil at FNB, a 2-1 Ian Wright inspired England at Old Trafford,a 2-1 loss to France and a 3-0 defeat to Germany.

The irony is that France had played against serious opossition like Russia, Sweden, Germany, Morocco and Finland amongst others while the Danes had also played Cameroon, Scotland, Norway and Sweden, all world cup material.

Saudi Arabia as shown by their mediocre performances, had only played other weak teams such as Namibia, Jamaica, Trinidad and Tobago amongst others. This did not go down well with a lot of supporters. Some however felt that South Africa was on the learning curve and that the 2002 Asia world cup would be much better.

South Africa is well aware that Doctor Khumalo is a professional sportsman with a serious amount of respect for the game. He did not cause a scene for the coach's lack of appreciation of his talent at the 1998 world cup. The team generally appeard to be disgruntled. They were indifferent. This was shown by intermittent individual performances at the world cup. The body language in the friendly matches prior to France 98 was also symbolic. The fact is that SAFA had created this situation by sacking Barker, a coach who had done so much for the nation and in whom the country believed. The coach who had so much understanding of his players. A cheap coach in terms of remuneration, also who knew both the strengths and weaknesess of the players. A coach who respected all his players. Barker was a coach who was also respected and understood by his players.

Many people wondered why SAFA looked further afield when there was Gordon Igesund-without doubt South Africa's most successful coach who has won several league honours with many local teams.Igesund himself had not applied for the job. His contention was that the position of National Team Coach should not be applied for, but that SAFA should simply call a coach they prefer, interview him,negotiate remuneration and agree terms. Basically, give that candidate the job if you believe he is the right one.Simple as that. A section of soccer lovers felt that Jomo Sono should have been given the job based on his 1996 and 1998 contribution,his record as a local coach and a shrewd talent scout. Another plus for the two was that, they understood the play pattern, the mentality, the culture and technique of local players more than any other coach from abroad.

"Philippe was good, but he was too confrontational," Doctor Khumalo told Kickoff.

Barker had been quite good to many a players. He had developed a rapport with almost all his players.Roger De Sa wrote in his book Man of Action, that Clive Barker would say to Doctor "when you have the ball, do some of your tricks on the ball, like rolling your feet over the ball, get the crowd buzzy and give them something to cheer, so they get on our side."

According to Roger De Sa, Clive Barker wanted players to replicate what they did at club level at the national team too. De Sa says Clive Barker surely got the best out of Doctor Khumalo. This is the type of coach that Doctor Khumalo liked and needed in his team.Philippe came across as a strict and harsh coach to most players despite the infamous 98 world cup night club scandal which involved the hugely gifted Naughty Mokoena and Brendon Augustine. The two players reportedly went out on a drinking bout and breached the team curfew. The two players were sent home the following day. Both players' careers later suffered. The two players plunged into obscurity. We have hardly heard of them since.

(7)

Post-France, 1998

In 1998, Doctor Khumalo, South Africa's most enterprising midfielder since the late Pule Ace Ntsoelengoe, lost his position in the national team! It must be stressed that Khumalo was something of a cult figure. His popularity at the time was not only widespread in the country but also across the African continent. His dropping caused a furore across the football divide. That did not bother coach Jomo Sono. Jomo is considered by many as South Africa's equivalent of Pele. During his heyday, Jomo Sono had an illustrious career with Orlando Pirates and New York Cosmos in the United States where he played with the great Pele. The respect that South Africa confers upon Jomo Sono is profoundly strong. He is renowned across the world for his phenomenal football exploits. He is also known in Africa for his business acumen. Jomo has accumulated a fortune through his athleticism and football prowess. His big name and brand have helped him navigate the business world. He was recently honored by the University of London with an Honorary Doctorate. Dr Jomo Sono has served Bafana Bafana as a Coach on several ocassions. He is largely regarded by many as the best talent scout in the country. His belief in youth development is both legendary and emperic. His football business model at Jomo Cosmos is quite simple. It is to develop ordinary players into great players. Then he sells them to European clubs. Back to 1998. When Jomo Sono took over Bafana Bafana, he introduced a brigade of youngsters, notably Quinton Fortune, who went on to play for Manchester United; Benni McCarthy of Ajax Amsterdam, who later played for, amongst others; Celta Vigo, FC Porto, Blackburn Rovers and West Ham United. Jomo Sono also introduced Aaron Mokoena who also plied his trade at Ajax Amsterdam and later at Portsmouth and Blackburn Rovers in the English Premier League. So, when a national hero of Jomo Sono's stature dropped another national hero like Doctor Khumalo from the national squad,not many people could stand up and argue. In fact, most people simply complained in the corridors. I must admit that it was a very difficult time in my life. I had never imagined Bafana Bafana without Doctor Khumalo. Never ever. That appeared to be the end of Doctor Khumalo's influence in both the squad and also in the sports pages of the South African media. I was terribly wrong! Doctor Khumalo had been the architect, the schemer-in-chief, the maestro, the thought leader and the indispensable figure in the Bafana Bafana midfield for the past six years. With Jomo Sono at the helm of the team, a new era had begun. Remember that very few people in South Africa can question Jomo Sono. Dr Jomo Sono is to South Africa what Franz Beckenbauer is to Germany. Jomo's football opinion is treated as gospel truth. To be blunt, one would not be wrong to suggest that Jomo Sono is by and large the face of South African football. But now, the South African football landscape had dramatically changed when no one expected it to change. But with or without Doctor Khumalo, life had to go on.

"I had sleepless nights thinking who I should take with between Doctor and Shoes. But in the end, I had to go for hard work and pace," Jomo Sono told the media.

This was during the announcement of his AFCON squad which went to Burkina Faso to play the 1998 edition of the most popular African cup tournament.

Doctor Khumalo had always conceded that he has never been a quick player, from his youth days throughout his professional career.

"Its unfortunate that people always talk about my lack of pace. Jomo Sono left me out of the squad last year for that very reason. If you ask people who saw me when i was still a reserve player, they will tell you that I was never a fast player. I have done a lot compared to the many players who have this much vaunted pace, but that's me.The same pace from the beginning and I will retire playing at the same pace I had when I started out," Khumalo responded.

It was clear that Jomo Sono wanted to have a look at new players-keeping a few of the old guard like Lucas Radebe, David Nyathi and Shoes Moshoeu. South Africa had been stunned by Clive Barker's unceremonious departure from the squad after the Confederations Cup. They would later be puzzled by Jomo Sono's 'infamous statement' that his selection criterion would not be influenced by crowd pullers and fan favourites. For many of us who had been in football for long, Jomo Sono's statement was unambiguous. Doctor Khumalo would not make the squad!

"I have been given a massive responsibility to lead this nation to greater heights therefore my selection would not be based on fan favourites. Every single player will have to work their way into the squad,"Sono said in his first Press Conference as Bafana coach.

It was Trott Moloto who recalled Doctor Khumalo back to the national set up. Doctor Khumalo would lead a largely inexperienced Bafana Bafana team to the Caribbean. The team was quite inexperienced with the exception of dreadlocked mercurial midfielder Thabo Mngomeni and the hard-running Sundowns forward Daniel Modau. They set off to the Carribean Islands of Trinidad & Tobago and neighbouring Jamaica. Doctor Khumalo had been out of the national team for some time. Although he had a sterling performance as captain on the tour, his teammates were rookies, they looked unsettled. Most of them were virtually nervous in the two encounters. Fabian McCarthy, Papi Mbele, Junaid Hartley were some of the new Bafana Bafana players on the Carribean trip. On their return, a new coach was subsequently appointed and another dramatic turn of events occurred.

(8)

The Pretty Boy

In Western society, beauty cspccially of women was defined as long straight hair, a fresh smooth face, slender physique and eyes as sparkling as the morning dew. Not all of this Doctor Khumalo had. Doctorson Theophilus Khumalo, very thin then in the neighborhood in Dube had lots of these in him. Doctor Khumalo's saunter was always noticeable. This is way before young old and contemporaries knew such word existed. Forget slow motion. Legend has it that time stood still when Doctor Khumalo walked down the streets or the corridors of Daliwonga High.He was a perfect example of a smart high school boy, admired by an avalanche of females and his school mentors mostly for his looks and his wizadry skills on the ball. It was not even for his school work neither. From time immemorial Doctor Khumalo has been a jeans freak. Mam' Mable would buy him Sharpeville modelled suits. Doctor Khumalo would only try them on and on a Sunday when mam' Mable expected the young boy to get to wear a suit. He would be there in jeans. He paid more attention to his hair than many of his contemporaries. It later appeared at Kaizer Chiefs that he would introduce the latest hairstyles. Shoes Moshoeu had an upper hand in hairstyles though. Dr Victor Ramathesele told those who had gathered at Shoes Moshoeu funeral that Shoes was a hair freak. Like Doctor Khumalo, he also loved sports cars but also collected vintage cars. Moshoeu always had these creative styles whenever he turned out for Bafana. I did not like or understand the hairstyles. But he lived in Europe. He was more advanced than many of his teammates. The hairstyles Shoes had then are the in thing today. The mohowks, some with different colours. This has since become a way to notice players today. Look at Paul Pogba at Manchester United today. Keagan Dolly at Bafana Bafana today. But also look at Makalakalane then!Doctor Khumalo has always been pedantic about how he looks particularly his hairstyles and dress sense. He truly understands the psychology of good looks. He never disappointed the showbiz when it came to what he wears to public events. Benni McCarthy often singles himself as the best dressed soccer player in South Africa.I do not quite disagree with Benni McCarthy but Doctor Khumalo is certainly one of the best dressed South Africans. Not just in football but generally. Kaizer Motaung Jr and Morgan Gould too. Doctor Khumalo regularly graces magazines for his expensive and suave dress style and so did Shoes Moshoeu. Doctor Khumalo has an appetite for designer clothes. In one of the interviews, he said he loved expensive suits from Italy and France.He truly has a seriously compelling dress sense. When Doctor Khumalo came to Botswana in 2010, I hosted him. Right from the plane, that morning, he was dressed to the nines. He looked suave, smelling exceptionally good. His wife at the time, Blanche Garises told me that Doctor Khumalo was well looked after by his personal sponsors especially Puma. Everything he wore on that day was Puma! When we fetched him from Sir Seretse Khama International Airport, I noticed something interesting. He wore a Puma watch, a Puma cap, a Puma tshirt and had Puma travel bags. The wife's luggage was also Puma! His relationship with Puma is a strategic symbiotic relationship dating back to 1987, Doctor Khumalo said to me. He wears Puma boots when training or playing testimonial or legends matches. Puma as his personal sponsor, pays Doctor Khumalo a handsome amount of money. And they dress Doctor Khumalo quite well.

Sitting together at the Grand Palm Hotel, by the pool side, Doctor Khumalo told me that his relationship with Puma started when he first signed for Kaizer Chiefs as far as 1987!

"Puma has been looking after me since day one of my professional career. They have really been very good to me."

Doctor Khumalo continues to be a hit in universities, colleges, mine hostels, train stations, bus stations and shopping centres in South Africa.His pictures and posters are synonymous with these places. He has also done commercials for various products and graced big billboards across the country. In the process, Khumalo is handsomely remunerated because of his star power. His looks and enterprising skills on the field of play equally made a fortune for him. When I was young, MTN had a very interesting advert with Doctor Khumalo playing with the ball before while answering a phone call. That advert intrigued many of us youngsters. I mean how many footballers would be able to play ''tep tep'' with the ball, yet still being able to take a phone call! Itumeleng Khune,Teko Modise and Siphiwe Tshabalala have also done remarkably well in commercial circles. Lucas Radebe too. Benni McCarthy could have done a lot of endorsements here but has hardly lived in South Africa since he left the country for Europe as an 18-year-old boy. So Benni McCarthy made almost all his fortune in Europe.McCarthy came back for two seasons and played for Orlando Pirates. He then moved back to Scotland where his wife Stacey Munroe resides with their daughter Lima Rose. Today,McCarthy is back in Cape Town where he is Head Coach of enterprising Cape Town City. For his big name, McCarthy is personally sponsored by Nike and Jaguar amongst others.

Below is a letter published in Soccer news written by one Tshepo Malaza of Ogies to his idol Doctor Khumalo.

"The boy who appeared with you in that lovely Coca Cola commercial, is he your younger brother or not. I am asking because some people claim that he is your child! Also, with your killer looks, why are you not taking part in TV serials as an actor?"

Khumalo responded in his column as follows." The little boy in that delightful commercial is not my child, nor is he my younger brother. He is just my neighbor. Well, as for taking part in stage or television acting, i think it is a natural progression after I've done a couple of commercials. If the right script and part come along, I'll seriously consider it."

Again, he dodged his looks comment by Tsepho, something he has always dodged on many occasions. Again, he would not mention anything about his family. The philosophy being what he does off the field or his personal life should not be mixed with football. This has worked quite until he quit soccer after 17 years of an illustrious football career.

Puma, probably because of the mileage and publicity they derived from Khumalo's popularity, decided to design a boot for the soccer star. This was well received by millions of youngsters across the African continent. I had an opportunity to visit Bulawayo in 2000 and the number of soccer boots I saw in the city centre engraved 16v was too much. At my own Primary school in Botswana, i remember that my school head Mr Lopang brought us all Doctor 16v Khumalo engraved boots! All new, all under the Doctor 16v Khumalo brand. Later as I was growing up, i realized that Doctor Khumalo was a huge brand, a commercial asset. Many players across the country used the 16v boots. It did not matter if it was Nico United or Mochudi Rovers in Botswana or Nkana Red Devils in Zambia or a player in a South African club either at amateur level or professional level. There was an obvious hype about the boots. I guess most of us thought we could become a Doctor Khumalo or even better than him. Some wore them simply out of respect and admiration for the star. Khumalo continues in his retirement Puma ambassador. He is always wearing something Puma. His relationship with the brand continues to grow from strength to strength. The other well-known personality with a long-standing sponsorship with Puma in South Africa is Jomo Sono. Jomo is a world-renowned soccer legend. To this his day Jomo Sono still reigns supreme as South Africa's King of soccer. He too, had boots called Jomo Sono King. Jomo is considered by many as the greatest South African soccer player of-all-time. This debate to me, gets more interesting as the years go by.

(9)

16 Valve

Kaizer Chiefs was formed in 1970 after a number of players from Orlando Pirates were not happy with management style at Pirates.Kaizer Motaung in particular, upon his arrival from United States where he had starred for Atlanta Chiefs convinced his team mates at Pirates that the situation had gotten out of hand that it was no longer possible to return to Pirates. Plans were hurriedly made to register the team but at the end Kaizer Eleven was formed. It later changed to Kaizer Chiefs in 1970. The same year, the team was allowed to participate in the mainstream league. It started recruiting the best players in the league and became a force to be reckoned with. Today, Kaizer Chiefs is the biggest supported club in the country with over 16 million registered membership. They are second only to the Springboks, the national rugby team in terms of popular appeal.

Amakhosi have won many more accolades than any other club in South African history. They have been consistently voted the best or at times-the second-best sports brand in the coutry in the same league with Springboks, the famous national rugby team that won the 1995 Webb Ellis Cup in South Africa. The Springboks also won the 2007 World Cup held in France.

Socrates Sampaio de Sousa Viera de Oliviera was a Brasilian soccer icon who retired in 1990 after failng to win a world cup with Brazil.He was a revered soccer icon in his homeland. He was tall, gangly with Bohemian beard and scruffy hair. Doctor Khumalo, who would later adopt Socrates as his popular nickname among the Chiefs faithfuls, was almost similar to the great Socrates. Except for the Bohemian beard that was Socrates trademark, the tall and ganly figure that is Doctor Khumalo is characteristic of the Brazilian legend. In addition to his incredible ball skills and guile, Doctor Khumalo, always, always had the crowd as his additional plus in his game. Doctor Khumalo was simply liked by supporters. Some within the opposition, while some were on their respective seats on the stands.

Today Doctor Khumalo still gets an applause when he enters the field as a player in an exhibition match or benefit match. He is very close to his fans. He often stresses that it is fans who always made him play well. His touches, the deftness, the deception in his movement and control, were always his strength. His body would shift with the ball, with an incredible tactical awarenes that in many incidents won both Bafana and Kaizer Chiefs many important matches. One match that comes to my mind is a match against Congo. He took a Congolese defender to the near corner. Doctor Khumalo slowly controlled the ball close to his feet, he faked a cross, the defender embarrassingly jumped only for Doctor Khumalo to roll his educated right foot on the ball. He did it twice! The poor defender danced to his tune. The late Phil Masinga had made a clever run into the box with other Bafana players. They waited rather hopelessly not thinking Doctor would whip a long cross right onto Masinga's path. Masinga did not disappoint. The Bari striker headed home a goal to put South Africa in the lead. In a Legends match against German legends in Limpopo in 2012, live on television, Doctor played a game of his life. He could do anything and everything with the ball. He was incredible. Doctor Khumalo brought back all my Junior High school's memories when I used to watch him do wonders. It was a truly nostalgic moment.

Doctor Khumalo was also good in taking long shots. He also had a very sharp eye for a decisive pass. Some people considered him a luxury player unwilling to work hard, reluctant to make tackles. Barker however, saw him as an intergral part of his team. Together with the mercurial Shoes Moshoeu, they made South Africa play with style and sophistication. Shoes would at times accelerate the match with his pace, while Khumalo would slow the match intentionally as a decoy, before unleashing a dangerous pass that leads to a goal. That was all calculated based on the way the opposition played. It is still an argument that Khumalo's play dictated how many goals South Africa could score in a match.

Doctor Khumalo did not have the physique of Jay Jay Okocha, nor did he have the speed of Steve Lekoelea or Jabu Pule.He had the genius of Okocha and certainly had the passion for the beautiful game. Khumalo was not like the late Thomas Madigage i grew to like, nor was he a replica of Aime Pablo of Argentina.Doctor Khumalo was not as quick as Thomas Madigage, Helman Mkhalele, Joseph Ngake or Ronaldinho. However, he compensated this weakness with his great passes. He never had to run his lungs out even when his team was under attack. Even when the situation was desperate. Doctor Khumalo would just dribble, hold onto the ball as much as he could and create space for his team mates. Sometimes he would even wait for a teammate to make a run and unleash a long intelligent pass. Simple as that. That worked for South Africa and Kaizer Chiefs. Smooth operation. That worked for Clive Barker.

I always compare the way in which Khumalo operated in midfield to the way that Raymond Ackerman anchors the retail game. The billionaire grocer is at the helm of a popular store Pick n Pay which he founded in the 60s. Ackerman is a prudent, shrewd businessman who worked tirelessly and quietly, amassing wealth with unmatched dedication, belief and patience. Khumalo is no exception in how much he invested in his talent.He had the talent and made sure that it was nartured and moulded into a finished product.The finished product would then make him a professional footballer who is respected across the world. Comparing Khumalo with titans such as Ackerman is certainly no exaggeration in the way he was able to sell his brand. The Doctor Khumalo brand is a long inspiring story. According to me, Doctor Khumalo should be used in colleges and universities particularly in marketing classes as a guest lecturer on brand management and marketing. Ackerman is respected worldwide for his business acumen. He perfected and packaged the Pick n Pay brand to millions of consumers. He applied himself and dedicated his life to the brand. I would say the same about Chris Wiese of Shoprite. This is a smart seller who sold the Shoprite story from Parow in Cape Town into

Africa through to the Middle East. Dj Sbu is another fantastic marketer, an organic marketing intellectual. The way he sells his brands to the masses is inconceivable. He has sold big brands and artists such as Zahara and Mzekezeke to revellers. DJ Sbu founded Mofaya energy drink under difficulty and supersonic media storm. The drink is the only 100% black owned African energy drink and has now flooded African markets. This, he did with chutzpah and passion despite facing a hurdle in doubting thomases. As a DJ, Sbu may not be as naturally gifted as global house superstars such as DJ Fresh,Black Coffee or Euphonik, but has sold his art quite convincingly. Dj Sbu is a shrewd marketing personality who is able to swiftly navigate circumstances and align his brand(s) with today's demands and dynamics. This is just what Doctor Khumalo has done in football business. He and his brand have never been irrelevant. Doctor Khumalo has sold his brand creatively to people even those who do not like soccer. This is the kind of talent one can not be apologetic about. We must always give credit where credit is due. Another thing is that Doctor Khumalo on the field always shone more against big opposition such as Moroka Swallows, Orlando Pirates, Sundowns and even Amazulu. He made it a point. This made him talk of the town. For many years.

Against Swallows, skillful players like Thomas Hlongwane, Andries Mpondo and Joseph Rapelego knew the kind of quality they were faced with in Doctor Khumalo.Having made his professional debut against the Mighty Bucs, Khumalo made sure Chiefs enemy number one always struggled. Just before they retired, Pirates defenders like Brendon Silent and Willem Jackson struggled to keep up with his antics, guile and deception.

Khumalo had a tight and personal control on the ball. Added to that was a highly perceptive passing ability. He also often unleashed a thunderous shot which often caught goalkeepers unaware. He had an incredibly delicate first touch and was without doubt a massive control inspiration behind Bafana Bafana victory in the 1996 Afcon.

Clive Barker has never hidden his admiration for Doctor Khumalo. His views on Doctor Khumalo were always in the public domain prior to the 1996 Afcon victory. Barker had told the media that albeit he had a strong, in tact, hungry and experienced squad, Doctor Khumalo was the pillar and the master behind the domination of the tournament. Fast paced Frank Amankwah of Ghana was silenced during the tournament. Amankwah was a stocky attacking left back with explosive acceleration. When Doctor Khumalo had the ball, he was devastating. He dismantled renowned Ghanaian left-back Amankwah with his skill on the flank. South Africa beat the much-fancied Ghana team which included Abedi Pele and his younger brother, Kwame Ayew.

In 2007, I met Abedi Pele Ayew. I asked him about the 1996 Afcon and Doctor Khumalo in particular. How he felt about the midfielder and what made him tick. Abedi Pele was categorical.

"We all knew about him long before the match. We had watched him during the tournament but you see players like that are special. Doctor was supremely gifted and to be honest with you he always had that deceptive control and dribbling talent which helped him take on defenders. It was sad to see us go down to them like that. But it is difficult to contain players like that the entire match when they are playing in their backyard with so much support behind them."

The former Marseille midfield kingpin was full of praise for Doctor Khumalo and the 1996 Afcon team. Ayew told me he had never seen South Africa so united and felt that if they were united and organized in 2010, then they could cause a surprise.

"The spirit of 96 was incredible for South Africa, but there was no consistency in terms of the structure post players like Doctor, Shoes, Fish and Lucas.South Africa should be able to produce another Doctor, Fish, Benni or Shoes. Unless a similar or better plan than the one of 1996 is used. Who knows? There may be suprises in 2010,"

While South Africa seemed to be enjoying their game during the tournament more than any other team. Doctor, Shoes together with Eric Tinkler would later get praise from another Pele. This time, Pele the great Brasilian.

"Doctor, Eric and Shoes are unbelievable players, i think they played their hearts out. They really made the difference in this tournament." Pele told Kickoff

Moshoeu played his heart out in the tournament. He was at his best ever for South Africa.He found that Khumalo had just come back from Argentina and had just rejoined the weakest Kaizer Chiefs ever.The Chiefs team of 1995//1996 was probably the worst team when one looks at the players of that season.It could not compete hence an unfashionable Manning Rangers won the inuagural PSL honours.Khumalo was fortunate because he had been doing well in Argentina for Ferro Carill Oeste before returning to South Africa. Shoes was ironically not doing well in Turkey. His form had taken a deep. Barker nevertheless kept him in the Afcon squad.

"1995 wasn't a good year as far as Kaizer Chiefs were concerned. Honestly we just didn't have a good team so we struggled all the way." Doctor Khumalo said.

(10)

The brand, DKSA

For me,Doctor Khumalo encapsuates all that which is beautiful about the beautiful game.It is opportune for me to divert a bit from Doctor Khumalo on the field, to take stock and anaylse his financial and brand proportions. I fully understand that his fans would like to know much about what their star makes a month or a year. It is with pity that i was never lucky to have those figures from the reliable sources i interviewed and during research. The other fact is the concerned companies themselves would never have divulged such confidential information to me. However, it must be stated that it is public knowledge that what Doctor Khumalo touches turns into gold. For example, when he married Blanche Garises in 2007, the media reported that a Namibian publication paid the couple over a R500 000 in total for their wedding rights! That is for exclusive interview and pictures of the wedding respectively. Whether that is true or not remains a matter of discussion for another day. Doctor Khumalo is without doubt among the richest sportsmen in South Africa. The media often speculates that his net value of assets stands at $5000, 000, 00. He may not be on the same earning perks with the likes of Lucas Radebe, Benni McCarthy or Ernie Else but Doctor Khumalo has certainly made a reasonable amount of fortune off the game. He has a number of professionals close to him like Percy Adams, *Advocate* Themba Langa and Cedrick Ramabulana. They have been behind the brand Doctor Khumalo for many years. They are probably behind the lucrative deals which have made Doctor Khumalo a big brand on and off the field. I assume that, in future-when the legend looks back on his professional career, he will have very little or no regrets about his financial investments. Themba Langa is a top legal eagle whose interest in sports law has risen over the years. He has helped wealthy clubs such as Kaizer Chiefs in litigation and soccer related transactions. In 2001, there was a widely publicized maintenance case brought about by one Zoleka Languza of Cape Town against Doctor Khumalo. A year later, in 2002, the South African Revenue Services (SARS) were on the star's case for alleged unpaid taxes amounting to over R2 million which related to Doctor Khumalo Close Corporation. These made newspaper headlines but both cases were nicely taken care of, thanks to the people around the brand Doctor Khumalo.

Doctor Khumalo has a number of sponsors and partners who date back to the early 90's. The latest partnership is with Sportpesa, a Pan-African but global gambling and betting company with interests in sports. Sportpesa has a footprint that stretches from East Africa to Cape Town to the English Premier League. In South Africa, innovative football supremo John Comitis introduced this enterprising brand when he launched his club Cape Town City in 2016. Doctor Khumalo is actively promoting this brand in South Africa and the region. He is handsomely paid for his image rights. Doctor Khumalo has probably enjoyed more positive mileage than any other sportsman in history of South African sports. Doctor Khumalo has a very solid, established relationship with Puma. Puma looks after their assets quite well. In Gaborone, Khumalo's wife at the time, Blanche Garises briefly told me about how Puma looked after the star.

"They really look after him. Everything is Puma, including the wife's bags," Blanche Garises told me with a giggle. Doctor Khumalo's relationship with Puma has been on going since i first got to watch him in the early 90's. However, he briefly wore Adidas boots when he was with Columbus Crew. That stunned his supporters not only in South Africa but also in Botswana. For some reason, when I met Doctor Khumalo, I was never able to ask him about that Adidas boot because he told me his relationship with Puma dated back to 1987. It's a relationship based on loyalty and respect for each other.

I was at Meepong Junior Secondary School in the Copper-Nickel mining town of Selibe Phikwe in Botswana when Doctor Khumalo was plying his trade in the United States.I remember a close friend of mine Thebeyame Obusitse rushing to me just before a Science class. Obusitse had with him the latest Kickoff edition. In that edition, Doctor Khumalo was wearing Adidas boots! We had a silly argument about it. My bone of contention was that his sponsorhip deal with Puma had probably come to an end while another funny classmate, Snow Pitsonyane who seemingly lacked basics about football made us bring the whole class into a mayhem. Obusitse would engage in a heated debate with Lucas Modimana whose sarcastic view was that "Doctor Khumalo is finished" and that Puma had decided against renewing his contract. Lucas was a profusely intelligent student ahead of many of his peers. He probably knew more and better about Khumalo's sponsorship than all of us. Lucas, I would later find out, was just in his comical element. He would later fuel a seemingly unnecessary debate either to ultimately get us expelled from class or cause a fight with those who could not comprehend football or bluntly, those that were ignorant thereof.

That is genuinenly the impact that Doctor Khumalo had on many of us. The arguments would go on until some 'experts' from other classes like Chillies Mogomotsi were called on to give their thoughts on the matter. Luckily on most occasions, i would be on the winning side as most students generally liked or knew Doctor Khumalo. This is despite the fact that they knew or did not know what the subject in detail, was all about.

My maternal uncle Shoti Sikwane is principally the man who made me respect Doctor Khumalo that much. He would always make sure i watched Doctor Khumalo especially against Orlando Pirates, Swallows and Sundowns.Sometimes, i would watch Doctor Khumalo play against Amazulu. Amazulu then,were a strong side which had an unprecedented support from Kwazulu-Natal.Doctor Khumalo did incredibly well against these sides and his personal brand grew from strength to strength. Literally so. His popularity swelled to unprecedented numbers. In Botswana, people started naming exceptional players after Doctor Khumalo while some simply named their children or a tukshop after him. It was not only in Botswana. It was worse in the townships of Soweto.I have been to the city of Bulawayo in Zimbbabwe a few times. There, I saw with my own eyes just how much Doctor Khumalo meant to football people. I remember at a mall in Nkulumane location where I had accompanied a friend of mine Mqondisi Dube, now sports Editor of Mmegi newspaper in Botswana.A hawker called ''Doctor'' wanted to know why I was not buying a match ticket from him.It looked like there was a match between Dynamos and Highlanders that afternoon.At the time, I was not even thinking that I would one day be working in Africa as a professional soccer agent, so I was not interested in Zimbabwean football. All I knew and was interested in, was the Zimbabwe national team which included the likes of Bruce Grobbler, the three Ndlovu brothers, Vitalis Takawira, Rahman Gumbo, Mercedes Sibanda just to mention a few.

Respected football legend Shaun Bartlett rather truly commented recently that the lack of quality strikers in the South African league is by and large caused by the fact that during his era, Doctor Khumalo and Shoes Moshoeu-both midfielders,were the only heroes to many a youngster.

"All these youngsters playing in the PSL today, grew up wanting to be like Shoes Moshoeu and Doctor Khumalo, hence we find ourselves having a problem of quality strikers in our league," said Bartlett.

Doctor Khumalo soon launched a pair of sunglasses which became a hit in the streets of Johannesburg. They also became popular in Botswana, Lesotho, Zimbabwe and Swaziland as well. In Kickoff magazine, Doctor Khumalo had a column wherein readers asked him questions about anything. His responses made some of us buy the magazine religiously. He had a palpably huge fan base and goodwill throughout Southern Africa. Consequently, he and his managers decided to start a Doctor Khumalo fan club. In the fan club, supporters stood a chance to meet him on his free time. They even won some mechandise from his wide range of goodies which also included the now popular sunglasses and caps. I would write letters from Selibe Phikwe in Botswana to Doctor Khumalo in Argentina via that fan club. One day he replied me in Kickoff, in the fan club. That response made me an overnight "celebrity" at Junior High School! I couldn't believe the amount of attention I got. It really made me develop more interest in Doctor Khumalo the player, and Doctor Khumalo the brand. It got very personal!

The fan club closed down after Doctor Khumalo left for the United States. A great deal of people really missed him much when he played in Argentina. Argentina seemed closed out for the media. While in the United States, Kickoff covered Doctor Khumalo a great deal. They even paid him a visit to cover him there. I also watched a few of his sublime skills in the MLS. Whenever he had a great game there, the SABC showed the glimpses in the news. Chiefs' fans were not used to Kaizer Chiefs playing without Doctor Khumalo. To them it was bizarre. Argentina was never going to work. It was just too far and too insular for someone whose career has always been a spectacle, a cheered one. Doctor Khumalo's game, from day one was premised on the support of his team mates and the support in the stands. Unfortunately, or rather fortunately, Argentina did not work out, and 16v returned home to South Africa after just six months. However, the love for Doctor Khumalo remained the same. Nothing changed. The fans welcomed him back. Kaizer Motaung recalled the player after it became clear that the Argentine club was failing to honor the agreed transfer fee agreement.

"Some people take it badly that I am one of the legends of South African soccer, but I have contributed a lot to the game over the last eleven years. I deserve to be remembered as one of the legends of South African soccer," Khumalo said.

He said this in an exclusive interview in 2000 with Sportslife magazine. He said this with regard to his illustrious career with both Bafana Bafana and Chiefs which at the time seemed to heading for the twilight.

"The capacity crowd that filled Vodacom Park is an indication of Khumalo's popularity. One will recall that at some stage during the mid 90's, the maestro (Doctor Khumalo) was second only to former state President Nelson Mandela in terms of popularity," Reginald Nkholise (Kickoff).

This coming from a highly esteemed writer like Nkholise, meant that indeed Khumalo was the undisputed new heir to the crown of South African soccer. To borrow Teko Modise's words "Doctor Khumalo was everything to the people of South Africa."

(11)

Doctor Khumalo (PTY) LTD

In 2004, Kickoff magazine announced that Doctor Khumalo had appeared on their cover pages than any other player locally. Esteemed soccer editor Richard Maguire showed appreciation for that when his publication rewarded the former star with an award at the magazine's 10-year anniversary celebrations held in Johanesburg. Today, maybe, just maybe, with the exception of Jomo Sono, it is probably safe to say that Doctor Khumalo remains the most popular sportsman to have come out of South Africa. Perhaps Mark Fish, McCarthy, Lucas Radebe, Siphiwe Tshabalala, Itumeleng Khune and Teko Modise may have have closed on the gap largely because they continued to play while Doctor Khumalo had long stopped playing at the end of 2002/2003 season. Doctor Khumalo is still popular across the country and in the neighbouring countries such as Zambia, Lesotho, Mozambique, Namibia, Zimbabwe and Botswana.He remains an icon that inspires multitudes of youngsters to date. Benni MCarthy is by far the most successful of the South African export players thus far. That also puts him in a better position. McCarthy played in the glamorous but intimidating English Premier League. He also played in Spain and Portugal thereby getting more international mileage and popularity.McCarthy rose to stardom at the 1998 Afcon in Burkina Faso when he scored 4 goals against neighbours Namibia in a 4-0 victory.He started off at the now defunct Seven Stars where he scored 37 goals in 28 matches in 1995/96 followed by 24 goals in 20 matches the following season; these exploits earned him a transfer to Cape Town Spurs in the PSL before he moved to Holland 's Ajax Amsterdam.He was later sold to Celta Vigo in the Spanish La liga before getting a move to Jose Mourinho's FC Porto in Portugal, with whom he won the Champions League.This is a colossal soccer resume which puts McCarthy in good stead in terms of accomplishments. But here is the difference between the two icons. McCarthy is a massively talented superstar whose goals inpired a great deal of youngsters in the Cape flats and around the country. This particularly in their bid to escape poverty and drug infested lifestyle synonymous with poor and idle African youngsters. But the blemish in Benni McCarthy's otherwise impeccable career is his outspokenness. He is usually very direct. He calls a spade a spade. Doctor Khumalo is relatively a conformist. McCarthy has always been in the media for either criticising SAFA for lack of professionalism or what he saw as unfair selection of players. The media often criticized him for being a prima-donna who often snubbed his country when he was having a good time at club level. He was once scolded for reportedly choosing to spend time with his Spanish-born daughters in Cape Town instead of playing for Bafana Bafana. Doctor Khumalo is a little different, rather diplomatic. He would never make ucomfortable statements about SAFA. He kept his family life completely out of the media when it was time to play for Bafana Bafana. That does not mean that Doctor Khumalo has always found SAFA to be good. A misunderstanding between Doctor Khumalo and SAFA arose when Khumalo was coach of South Africa U-17s. That relationship was startlingly short lived. The circumstances of that termination remain sketchy.

Doctor Khumalo might be over 50 years old now but continues to look good and suave in his suits. He is the same whether he is in track suits as coach of Kaizer Chiefs or TD at Baroka FC. He actually looks even nicer in casual wear. After all the years of chasing ball,his looks particularly his beautifully built body still mesmerises many a young woman. Like his father, Eliakim and the club boss Kaizer Motaung, Doctor Khumalo has developed a bald. I guess that's where his obsession with caps comes from. Perhaps to cover the bald. These days in his retirement, Doctor Khumalo prefers to have his head clean shaven. However,female fans continue to admire him. Many people still want to have a picture with the star or at the least get his autograph. He is still likeable to many. He remains very attractive to many women across the age and colour devide because he truly looks the part. Like very successful people especially sports stars and celebrities, Doctor Khumalo always smells very good. He wears very expensive colognes of exotic designer names.

During the early days of his fame, Doctor Khumalo exuded eyes radiating intelligence, his lanky looks and small frame (then) worked for him. Opponents would in most cases not notice him until when he recieved or released the ball and with a raucous cheering from them with his ball skills, *shibobos* and *tsamayas*. The clapping built into a crescendo, immediately after performing a magical stunt on the ball, Doctor Khumalo would in turn, smile affably to the fans and his bench. Doctor Khumalo would soon become an overnight icon amongst the Chiefs family. To the Motaung dynasty, he became their son. To South Africa, he remains the country's favorite son.

By a strange quirk of fate, Doctor Khumalo's close friend Teboho Moloi joined Orlando Pirates. This intensified the rivalry between the two friends on the field of play. Doctor Khumalo, an incredible ball player with intelligent quick-thinking mind, would in most cases emerge a victor against Teboho Moloi of Orlando Pirates. Tebza, as Teboho is affectionately known, was slow like Doctor Khumalo, but possessed an avalanche of ball antics and tricks which Pirates supporters loved to see him perform every match. He was somewhat reluctant when it came to showmanship. Teboho was a visionary with amazing passing ability and intelligent but authoritative ball control. While Khumalo's magic went on to help Bafana on many occasions, Teboho Moloi never really blossomed into an internationally acclaimed Bafana Bafana star like his closest friend. It could probably be because Moloi was confined to a relatively unknown Colombian league for most of his overseas career. At 20 years, Doctor Khumalo had the world at his feet after winning a cup with Kaizer Chiefs. A few years later in 1992, he won the coveted South African Player of The Year (Footballer of the Season) accolade. This was the beginning of great things-on and off the field-for South Africa's fastest emerging and enterprising black super star.

By 1992, Doctor Khumalo was the most famous player in South Africa. He became an indispensable figure in the Amakhosi line up. His influence in any match, like he was in the media pages, was equally visible.

Doctor Khumalo had played alongside the legendary Ace Ntsoelengoe, who played a meanigful role in developing Khumalo's self esteem and confidence as a player in the reserves and later in the first team. Ntsoelengoe passed on in 2005 from a suspected heart attack in Lenasia. His death came after Doctor Khumalo had just returned to South Africa after spending a week in England on a football trip with a popular Coca-Cola talent search project.He had said goodbye to Ace Ntsoelengoe a few days before he left for the UK. Khumalo in his own admission, said he had never thought that would be the last time he saw Ace Ntsoelengoe alive. Ace Ntsoelengoe together with a host of Chiefs family which retired just before 1990 played a very significant role in making, protecting, developing and refining Doctor Khumalo both as a player and a person. Ace Ntsoelengoe and Kaizer Motaung had played in the USA in their heyday. They had brought with them the suave American dress sense to Soweto, the bell bottom, tailored suits and hispanic bohemian hairstyles. Doctor khumalo did not only copy them on their amazing football acumen, the runs, the passes, the wit and the way they dazzled their opponents. The way Ace Ntsoelengoe dummied his opponents at the same time confusing and exciting his own fans. He, Khumalo-also took a leaf out of their dress book. Kaizer Motaung is a revered soccer boss with a unbelievable penchant for elegance, he is known for a refined dress sense.

Khumalo is still considered one of the best dressed sportsmen in South Africa. He is synonymous with class, sophistication and immaculate dress sense that includes impeccable designer clothes, expensive watches and fast sports cars. This could probably make Benni McCarthy jealous because Benni McCarthy like all world superstars likes really nice things. And he has, and affords them in abundance. I have seen him over the years. He is a superstar. Before his wedding in 2007, Khumalo was always linked by the media to very beautiful women. But as usual, his lovelife remained private. His subdued smile reflects his inner self. From my own experience, Doctor Khumalo is a somewhat shy but reclusive to people he does not quite know. He is therefore never in the press for mischivious acts against any body. In 2017, in the opulent suburb of Douglasdale, I found Doctor Khumalo dining in the VIP section of high-end restaurant Throbbing Strawberry with some people. He is a very private person who prefers to stay away from the limelight. Yes, Doctor Khumalo is certainly not perfect. No one is afterall. An almost impeccable 17-year long career almost got a blemish when allegations of unpaid tax emerged in 2002. SAPA reported that Khumalo was given a penalty and the charges were withdrawn. Kickoff magazine startlingly reported a furore with the late Shoes Moshoeu over a parking area at the Kaizer Chiefs village.This,they attributed to player star power. Kickoff magazine further reported a misunderstanding between Doctor Khumalo and the then goalkeeper coach and Swazi legend William Shongwe. Shongwe is one of the exceptionally gifted television soccer commentators in South Africa today. The widely reported accident story was however very bad for the brand Doctor Khumalo. It was widely covered by the media. Also, Zoleka Languza's maintenance claims fizzled out quickly after wide publication in Cape Town papers. These,to my knowledge, remain the only known blemishises to Doctor Khumalo's otherwise great professional resume as an outstanding athlete and a massive sports brand. Doctor Khumalo boasts a phenomenal football career and a fantastic ability to respect sponsors and partners. As I have stated before, Doctor Khumalo like any other person-can not be perfect, and is not perfect. What is noteworthy and rather commendable is that, his imperfections have not been able to embarass him as has been the case with some of the other big guys in sport around the world. Many people in the public eye have been drowned and finished off by scandals here in South Africa and elsewhere in the world. Khumalo's single status was and continued to be under harsh scrutiny and scathing attack until he married Blanche Garises.The questions that used to be asked, some even bizarrely directed to me personally were; when is he going to get married? Whom is he going out with? He's rich, who is going to inherit his wealth? Does he have kids? Unfortunately, I did not know the answers. I still don't know the size of Doctor Khumalo's bank account. But he has certainly done very well for himself. Besides the son Diego Khumalo, i only knew of his daughter Theonada Livin Khumalo. These have always been my answers to these bizarre questions from many of the people who understood my admiration for Doctor Khumalo. Unfortunately, 25-year-old Theonada passed away in July 2017 at a Johannesburg hospital after her VW Polo Vivo got involved in a bizarre accident. Doctor Khumalo majestically wrote a moving eulogy for his daughter in Soccer Laduma. "I saw my daughter when she was born, and I held her hand when she took her last breath," Khumalo wrote. I was devastated, like when Shoes Moshoeu passed on. When Shoes away, I felt that Doctor Khumalo would never be the same again. They had one of the best partnerships ever seen in African football. They were close. They shared hotel room during camps. When Doctor Khumalo described his relationship with Theonarda, it was more like the second Shoes had been stolen from him. It was touching. Riveting!

Doctor Khumalo was clearly lost for words talking about his first born. "She was full of love and she was a woman with a brave heart," Khumalo wrote.

These questions mostly came from females whose knowledge about Doctor Khumalo's bank account seemed to surpass their knowledge about the goals he scored for both Bafana Bafana and Chiefs. Like many of the superstars in Africa, he married outside the country. Samuel Eto married his beautiful wife Georgette Tra Lou of Ivory Coast and Didier Drogba's beautiful wife Alla Diakite is from Mali. Benni McCarthy's first wife was from Spain while the current one Stacey Munroe is from Scotland. Kalusha Bwalya's wife is South African Italian, Emmy Caselletti. This is a common trait amongst rich African soccer stars.

"I do not like talking about my private life in public. I want people to ask me about my football and not what i do besides soccer. However, there's that special person in my life," Doctor Khumalo said.

I guess that's the life of a star whose football ability and skills raised so many expectations about his life beyond the field. I guess it is only natural. It is not just Doctor Khumalo.

Another player who faced the same scathing scrutiny and criticism is the late Shoes Moshoeu whose private life remained private despite the oppulent lifestyle he lived. Shoes Moshoeu was by all accounts, a handsome soccer player. The obvious pressure of expectations followed. Shoes Moshoeu hardly opened up to the press or the public about family and other things beyond football. Most people were surprised to see Shoes Moshoeu's four beautiful children at his funeral in 2015. He preferred his life beyond soccer to remain private. The pressure on the so called celebrities is obscene. In African society, it is anomalous for a well off or rather a relatively rich man to remain single. The pressure is just too much for public figures like politicians and sports stars. Unfortunately, Khumalo has been no exception. The public waited, and waited. But Lucas Radebe, Mark Fish and Brian Baloyi took the lead in marriage early in their lives. Brian Baloyi married his beautiful wife Pungi Baloyi while he was still in his twenties. Mark Fish too. Fish married his wife Loui Fish while he was a youngster playing in Italy. Unfortunately, Mark Fish and Loui Fish divorced in 2011.

After Lucas Radebe's first wedding in 2004, all eyes shifted to Doctor Khumalo to walk down the aisle.

To many, Doctor Khumalo was a pretty boy who did not put much effort to play professional football in Europe. Europe, it seems, is the ultimate destination where everybody expected him to go based on his interminable talent. *Honorable* Botsalo Ntuane, a well-known politician in Botswana-is a big Jomo Sono fan whose South African football appreciation and understanding is supreme. *Honorable* Ntuane, in jest-often describes Doctor Khumalo as "just a handsome player." Ntuane reckons that Doctor Khumalo's good looks contributed immensely in "luring" ladies to the stadiums. He however insists that Doctor Khumalo is way below Jomo Sono in the perking order of great South African soccer stars. One leading magazine once wrote that

Doctor Khumalo failed to rise in stature to equal both Ace Ntsoelengoe and Jomo Sono. I think this is unfair. Khumalo played football in a different era from Jomo Sono's. Doctor Khumalo has amassed a reasonably good fortune from the game. Throughout his life, Doctor Khumalo has appeared in papers and on television displaying a glamorous life, a good life. People are inherently not destined for the same paths and successes in life. Black township boys looking at Doctor Khumalo's luxurious life of a big mansion in Fourways, fast, expensive sports cars and an expensive lifestyle in the northern surbubs is enough inspiration. That's motivation enough. But it would be unfair to compare Doctor Khumalo to a Benni McCarthy or Samuel Eto'o or Michael Essien in terms of wealth. Doctor Khumalo has driven almost every luxury car South Africa has ever offered. That's sufficient motivation for me and every black man who has known and faced adversity. That should be sufficient success in the eye of that youngster in Tsomo and Lusikisiki in the Eastern Cape, to the ambitious black entrepreneur in Galeshewe in Kimberly and to that aspiring soccer player in Montshioa township of Mafikeng. Doctor Khumalo means a great deal to black youngsters in Giyani, Phuthaditjaba and Umlazi. My own cousins in Mabeskraal and the ones in Old Naledi Township and Monarch in Botswana see Doctor Khumalo as the epitome of success. Doctor Khumalo's own homeboys in Dube in Soweto should really be spurred when they see the life that football gave him. 16v, as Doctor Khumalo is fondly known, is without a doubt a cult hero in Botswana. I know this. During my boyhood in Botswana, i played football.I know what Doctor Khumalo meant to the dreams of those friends I played with. I work with professional footballers in the the Absa Premier League, in Southern Africa, East and North Africa. I know how much Doctor Khumalo inspires boys in Africa. His glamourous life on television and magazines drove most of the boys to work harder in life. His fame and fortune could only accelerate the hunger in many of us. Take DJ Fresh as an example.Is there a DJ in Africa, particularly in Botswana and South Africa who is not or was not inspired by DJ Fresh? If yes, then that DJ is probably dishonest to the game. I literally know what DJ Fresh means to the people in music, especially those who don't sleep on their dreams. Dipsey Selolwane and Mogogi Gabonamong are up there on the football ladder because they watched Doctor Khumalo as small boys growing up in

Botswana. He inspired them. They too turned professional, ultimately. I once watched a TV show which showing soccer stars' lifestyles. It focused more on the players' cars and houses. It showed a glimpse of Doctor Khumalo's magnificent mansion in the splendid surburb of Fourways, north of Johannesburg. There was an interesting fleet of German sedans parked around; top of the range BMW 745i, BMW X5, BMW Z4 and AUDi TT Quatro! That is Doctor Khumalo for you. But truth be told, it seems like Khumalo was relatively better off than most of his peers growing up. His mother Mable Khumalo is now a retired school teacher. His late father Pro Khumalo, was a professional soccer player for Kaizer Chiefs. Being the last boy(born) in a family of two kids meant that Doctor Khumalo probably got the best out of his parents. He is from a middle-class Zulu speaking family in Soweto whose values are rooted in *ubuntu*. They are relatively ambitious family with strong emphasis on education and respect for people. That is how Doctor Khumalo has remained grounded and on the straight despite his fame and fortune. When Doctor Khumalo left the United States, he repeatedly stressed that part of the reason was to look after family businesses. It has however remained unclear as to what exactly the family businesses entail. Very few people with his fame and fortune are responsible enough to maintain this durability.

A lot of people think that Doctor Khumalo hardly really sweat for his fame and fortune. The truth is that Doctor Khumalo grew up in a close knit family which believed in hard work and education. This is symbolised by his own father Eliakim, who at the time of his death was Head of Development at Kaizer Chiefs. He enjoyed working with kids and was as fit as a fiddle. Eliakim worked for many years with Kaizer Motaung. He died at the hands of hijackers while still under the employ of the club. This demonstrates the loyalty and commitment of the man to his friend, Kaizer Motaung. So, Eliakim valued both friendship and family. Doctor Khumalo has not turned out to be different. He spent a memorable 31 years with Kaizer Motaung and the Chiefs family until recently when he switched to Baroka FC as a Technical Director. This move shocked and surprised a lot of people.

The truth is that Doctor Khumalo was very open to his parents and made sure that he made shrewd financial investments from an early age. Khumalo has been dabbling in business since the days of Paul Dolezar at Kaizer Chiefs.The maverick Yugoslav born- French speaking coach once told a publication that he would not rely on senior players like Brian Baloyi and Doctor Khumalo because they are businessmen!

"I can't rely on Doctor Khumalo and Brian Baloyi anymore. Doctor has 5 cars and 3 phones. He is in Durban now, maybe Cape Town tomorrow for business,"Dolezar said.

But what is more exciting is that Doctor Khumalo is a role model today. He serves as an inspiration to many a black boy across South African townships. He is a true, genuine and accurate embodiment of a black man who has attained his goals. He has certainly achieved and lived his life dreams and ambitions of self aggrandizement. I have had the pleasure of spending time with Doctor Khumalo. Listening to Doctor Khumalo, he is incredibly smart. I also noticed that he is very patient about life but still very ambitious. Doctor Khumalo wants to be a head coach in the future. Like Jomo Sono and Kaizer Motaung,he also wants to own a club.Ultimately. He is a visionary who believs in youth development because he is a product of school football himself. I have listened to him speaking about players such as Thabo Matlaba, Themba Zwane and those he has helped develop such as Lorenzo Gordinho and Siphosakhe Ntiya-Ntiya. I experienced this first hand listening to him. He is a very intelligent coach who emphasizes that coaches must always equip themselves with education. He does not believe that talent alone is good enough. He would not have gone to coaching coarses in Germany and the United Kingdom.

Doctor Khumalo grew up knowing that what his father had, belonged only to his father. He worked smart, and invested his money wisely. He has never had cars reposessed or a house put under the hammer. There is a common trait amongst successful black soccer stars who went on to amass wealth on the international stage with big clubs or with Bafana Bafana, and then plunge into poverty a few years into retirement. Examples are varied and many. It is not just a common South African story. A study in the USA showed that 68% of sports people get broke after five years in retirement-after hanging up their boots! It is also not just in football. This also happens in other fields such as music and politics. This phenomenon is devastatingly common within successful black elites who earned obscene amounts of money during their heyday. The result of driving fast cars, drinking Moet & Chandon and Ciroc every weekend at nighclubs escorted by hangers on. At the centre of this largesse and obscene indulgence is strangers and cunning but creative womenfolk whose purpose is to milk soccer stars dry. With these strangers, are the so-called friends who basically live off these stars without offering a single idea about investment and the future. These people run away to the next "star" when their "boy" gets into financial trouble. This is the painful truth that often visits our superstars in Africa. Fortunately, Doctor Khumalo has not made any headlines for such wayward lifestyle and prodigality.

(12)

Mdokies & The Dawg

The Dawg as is popularly known, is until today South Africa's most succesful coach at national team level. Born William Clive Barker, in 1944 in Durban, Clive is a one of the first generations of coaches with an English FA coaching badge. Clive is not really your typical coach in the literal sense of tactics and strategy. Those who know him better say he is the best manager in the world. He simply manages personalities. His players say he is extremely approachable and amicable. Barker has hardly coached top clubs in his entire coaching career. He has never managed Kaizer Chiefs, Moroka Swallows, Supersport United, Mamelodi Sundowns or Orlando Pirates.He has always been synonymous with Amazulu since 1974 as a coach. Amazulu is a professional Durban club which has had a fair share of ups and downs in its rather massive history as traditional pride for the soccer crazy Kwazulu-Natal Province. Amazulu are traditionally very strong in support. They have the Zulu nation, Africa's largest nation behind them in the Kwazulu-Natal.In the early 70's and 80's, Amazulu support was huge. I started watching Amazulu in the early 90's during the days of Joe Mlaba, George Dearnely, Simon Magagula and Shadrack Biemba. Another great player whom i did not see was Joel Fire, Amazulu's greatest player according to popular opinion. During Amazulu's great days, they competed fiercely with Amakhosi and Pirates but the latter's advantage would be that they have support across the country. Amazulu under Barker could also compete well. They beat top clubs and won silverware. They made history when they beat Kaizer Chiefs 3-1 in a Coca Cola Cup Final in 1992. This is despite the fact that Kaizer Chiefs had a star-studded team comprising of Doctor Khumalo, Lucas Radebe, Ace Khuse, Fani Madida and Shane MaGregor amongst others.

However, Amazulu have a sad history of getting relegated at times and later surfacing in top flight football. This i would contend is a result of inconsistency in ownership that characterised the team before the Sokhela family took over. The fact is that Clive Barker has a soft spot for the club. Retail giant Spar have always been associated with the club. Legend has it that Amazulu lose their Spar sponsorhip whenever the club relieves Barker off his responsibilities as a coach!His association with Amazulu is long and memorable to many. Some people had, or still have a right or wrong impression that Barker has a stake in the club. As in the case of Doctor Khumalo with Chiefs, many people have argued, quite steadfastly that Doctor Khumalo was and is a shareholder at Kaizer Chiefs.This, I have also heard in many conversations and debates about his association with the Chiefs empire. According to Bobby Motaung this is totally incorrect.

"Doctor has always been with the club and at some stage,he was looking at buying a stake in the club. That was not granted though," Bobby Motaung said.

There has also been a misconception amongst Arsenal fans who mistakenly thought that Arsene Wenger was a shareholder of the club. This misconception extended to Sir Alex Ferguson when many people said he would not leave Manchester United because he was a shareholder at the club! Both stories are altogether incorrect. I hope the reader fully understands what informed this misconception.

These are common untruths when a person has been with a company or an organisation for a very long time. This is just some of the illustrations that a brand can become synonymous with another to a point where people mistakenly believe untruths as facts. But the beauty of this untruth is the fact that, the loyalty of the brand to another is a genuine reflection of what the people's wishes are. Upon taking the Bafana Bafana job, Barker publicly said Doctor Khumalo would be an intergral part of his team. He made it categorically clear to the media and everybody who cared to listen.

DOCTOR KHUMALO SOUTH AFRICA

"I think he's the finest player in this country. I think Doctor Khumalo is gonna be part of my team for many more years to come. Which coach wouldn't want a player like him in his team? He's got the right attitude. He wants to learn and his ball skills and passes will surely take us somewhere."

The Chiefs fan's favourite would then make almost every team that Barker picked. He would continue to make more fans throughout South Africa and elsewhere in the world under Barker's tutelege. He was now better exposed to millions of soccer supporters across the continent with Bafana Bafana. He had won many accolades with the national team. To be quite honest, Doctor Khumalo is one of the few players i have known in my entire life, who is loved across team divide. One such player is Zinedine Zidane. Thiery Henry too. Of late, Mohommed Salah of Liverpool seems to be one such player. Ordinarily, a Pirates fan should have a problem with a Chiefs player. Its war. But with Doctor Khumalo, it is different. In fact, it appeared at least to me, that almost everybody in football loved Doctor '16v' Khumalo notwithstanding their team affiliation.

Barker's profile as a club coach was generally good, but the team he picked catapulted his name to a super league of coaches. There was a strong unity between players then. The essence was incredible. Players supported each other and respected the national team jersey. Plus both the flag and the badge. They all,together sang the national anthem with excitement and respect. Barker and Doctor Khumalo would form a very close relationship on and off the field. Clive Barker relied on Doctor Khumalo's special skills. Doctor Khumalo in turn, relied on Barker's motivation. The relationship was palpably reciprocal. This was absurd. Everybody in the Bafana team knew that Doctor Khumalo and Clive Barker were friends. The Team Manager, Glyn Binkin-Barker's closest friend,knew this too. They all knew why that relationship existed. But Barker respected all his players. Barker could nonetheless not hide his admiration for Doctor Khumalo.Barker said on numerous occasions that Doctor Khumalo resembled Ace Ntsoelengoe.So to Barker, Khumalo was his most important player. That was no secret. In the process of these victories, Barker became very popular in the country. The aeroplane-signature-celebration became popular within the streets and townships.He was very approachable and liked being close to supporters.He always explained his selection criteria well in time.I remember sometime in December in the late 90's, Barker said that he would be leaving out a midfielder for a match that would take place in Zambia in February the following year.He was open, fairly honest.In 2007, I bumped into Barker at Oliver Tambo International Airport in Johannesburg. I asked him a few questions about Shoes Moshoeu. They were both at Amazulu at the time. He answered all my questions. He was very protective of his players. There is a funny thing which i asked which he hurriedly and repeatedly said which taught me something about Clive. At the end of the conversation, i needed Shoes Moshoeu's mobile number for a business proposal I wanted us to work on together. Barker was not fooled.

"Ask Amazulu, please ask Amazulu my boy,"

I pressed for Shoes' email adress and Clive was straight foward

"Please phone Amazulu office. They will help you, ok."

That was the parting shot from Clive Barker. He is very steadfast at times and does not budge easily despite his amicable personality. SAFA would be better placed to tell just how strong-willed Barker was during their time together. Their relationship ended in controversial circumstances which have not been made public. Unceremoniously, out of the blue-Barker left SAFA House for good on the eve of the 1998 World Cup in France!

Barker is much of a motivator than a modern tactician who thrives on sophistry and technology. He is obviously from old school type of coaching discipline having started coaching in the 70's. At Bafana, he chose players purely based on form, talent, grit and commitment. His line up was common cause and predictable. We could easily predict it in class with my boys.

Starting in goal; Andre Arendse, Sizwe Motaung, David Nyathi, Mark Fish, Lucas Radebe, Eric Tinkler, Shoes Moshoeu, Doctor Khumalo, Phil Masinga, Shaun Bartlett and Helman Mkhalele. This starting line up stayed like this for many years. Mark Williams would come on from the bench, with John Moeti or Linda Buthelezi replacing Tinkler or Doctor Khumalo. Barker was never really an ambiguous person in his coaching philosophy and line up. When Doctor Khumalo's pace slowed, Clive Barker would often single out Shoes Moshoeu as his match winner. Shoes Moshoeu was Doctor Khumalo's closest friend in the team. They often shared a room together in camp especially at the Sunnyside hotel during the 1996 Afcon .

(13)

Argentina

Doctor Khumalo had probably never thought of playing his football in Argentina. He was well known in Africa. He was extremely popular in South Africa. And the agents around the world took notice. He caught the attention of revered FIFA agent Marcello Houseman. Houseman was a gifted negotiator but had a fair share of his own troubles. Khumalo placed his future, his talent in Houseman's hands. Houseman was to look for more lucrative opportunities for Doctor Khumalo around the world. Fortunately, or rather unfortunately, Houseman took Doctor Khumalo, South Africa's finest, most sought after, most talented star, most popular player to Argentina of all countries!

"Playing against Argentina was scary, they had such a big reputation. Fortunately we had Clive and he believed in us. He had emphasized to me earlier in the year that I was the man to make the team tick. Here at home nobody gave us a chance but we nearly beat them and I managed to score as well. That performance paved the way for me to join Ferro Carril Oeste in Benois Aires. In my opening game, I scored and our opponents had Burachagga who played with Maradona in the world cup and was still a respected guy in Argentina."

Doctor Khumalo also scored from an akward angle, one of the best goals I ever saw, against River Plate. He became talk of the town. He was a major hit in Argentina already. The media took interest in him. He had scored against a tough team, in a big match. Unfortunately, Doctor Khumalo came back home to South Africa after only six months! This was because the Argentines could not honour their financial obligations with Kaizer Chiefs supremo, Kaizer

Motaung over Doctor Khumalo's transfer fee. Kaizer Motaung recalled Doctor Khumalo- arguably the most valuable asset in club history.

"Ferro Carril were supposed to give Kaizer the whole amount for my transfer but after five months they had not paid fully. They had only paid half of it and Kaizer said I should come back. It was nice in Argentina but the other problem was the language. They had interpreters for me for team talks," Khumalo wrote in his Kickoff column

It was over with Argentina. Doctor Khumalo rejoined his Kaizer Chiefs teammates for another season in the National Premier Soccer League.

(14)

The American Dream

As a soccer fan, particularly Doctor Khumalo's, it was sad to see him leave for the United States.Amakhosi held a banquet for the player as a bye-bye to Ohio where he would link up with Columbus Crew.I think it is important to make mention of the fact that the US Soccer League had just started off in 1995. Most clubs were looking for fine players across the world. Pele the great, Jomo Sono, Frans Backenbauer and Kaizer had all played in the USA in the 60's and 70's. The momentum had long died down during their era. Now, the rich sports gurus such as the Hunt family in Texas had shown immense interest in soccer as a business.

Lamar Hunt is a Texan whose wealth and love for sports is well known across the US. Lamar Hunt had decided to go into soccer. He founded Columbus Crew. Lamar Hunt was born in 1932 and died in 2006 after succumbing to prostate cancer. Lamar was a renowned sportsman and promoter of American fooball, soccer, tennis, basketball and ice hockey. He would leave his wealth to his family who continue to be in the forefront of both Columbus Crew and Dallas FC with an astute grand son, Clark Knobel Hunt being the chairman of the Board of the National Football Leagues Kansas City Chiefs. Clark Hunt remains a founding investor owner in the MLS.Clark is a shrewd young man with remarkable business acumen with impeccable business qualifications.He is a respected sportsman-cum-businessman today in the United States.The MLS is the fifth biggest sports league in the United States,meaning that its not as massive as a sports code as it is in South Africa.The MLS is structured as a single,limited company and single entity in the single entity business structure.Club operators own a financial stake in the league itself,not just their individual teams.

The way the Crew is run is not totally different from Kaizer Chiefs, where Doctor Khumalo had been since 1985.In the Chiefs village today, there is Chairman Kaizer Motaung, his younger brother Cyril Motaung who is Supporters' Cordination Manager. Jessica Motaung who started off in the marketing office has now been co-opted into the Board of Directors and serves as Director of Marketing, fuelling speculation that she may succeed her father Kaizer Motaung as executive chairperson. Kaizer has also said that he would like to pave way for new generation with new ideas once Kaizer Chiefs stadium and radio station projects have been completed. This is clearly a feat he would like to achieve before his retirement. Then there's Bobby Motaung who's the club Football Manager. Bobby is the second most powerful person at Naturena. He is tasked with executive management of the team and links it with the board. I have met Bobby Motaung twice in my life-a suave dresser and a shrewd football man who understands African football so much. To be fair to Bobby Motaung, he has the most difficult job in South Africa. When the club wins trophies, supporters hardly give Bobby any credit. Supporters simply celebrate the coach and the players only when Chiefs win. When Chiefs go through a bad spell, the whole country descends on Bobby Motaung. The reasons may be attributed to what Bobby Motaung alledgedly said in the media when supporters called for his head. Bobby alledgedly said that he was employed at the club because he is Kaizer Motaung's son and that he did not get the job through a resume! And that the fans must live with it.Then there's his younger brother Kaizer Jr, a retired striker for the senior team who upon completion of A-levels at the prestigious Harrow School in England came back to play for his father's club. Before professional soccer, Kaizer Jr was a good cricket player having represented South Africa at junior levels.There is also the pleasant Kemiso Motaung who works as Digital Manager overseeing the club's social media space.She was previously with Jakes Productions-a separate but related arm of the Motaung empire which helped promote the annual Miss Kaizer Chiefs and other club events.So it is true that Kaizer Motaung's family will always be with Kaizer Chiefs even after his departure.This phenomenon has since spread to other clubs with Orlando Pirates supremo Dr Irvin Khoza who had his late daughter, Zodwa Khoza as Brand Manager. Khoza's sons Nkosana and Mpumi are also intimately involved at Pirates in their respective executive roles at Parktown. Jomo Sono also has all his four children involved at Jomo Cosmos. First-born Nyiko Sono is Brand Manager of the club while another daughter Randzo Sono-Masango serves as Chief Executive Officer of the club. The eldest son Bamuza Sono who recently retired from top flight football has since assumed the position of Team Manager.Last born Matsilele Sono is a rising star player at the club. Mike Mokoena, the founder of Free State Stars has his son Rantsi Mokoena as club General Manager while Farouk Kadodia has enlisted his brother's services at Maritzburg United. His son Younis Kadodia also works for the club. Ajax Cape Town is currently owned by the Efstathiou brothers Ari and Alexi while erstwhile owners were John and George Comitis with their father Mike Comitis also very involved. I am not sure if George Comitis is involved the same way at their current club Cape Town City where John Comitis is the supremo, who is clearly assisted by his three sons. I also noticed this trend at FC Cape Town where astute club owner Errol Dicks oversees the whole machinery while his sons Darren and Bevan Dicks were involved in some capacity. Darren Dicks played for the club while Bevan Dicks worked as a promising player agent. Lunga Sokhela is General Manager at Amazulu while his father Dr Patrick Sokhela is executive chairman of the club. Mato Madlala owns Golden Arrows and her daughter Nonceba Madlala is highly involved at the club. I found this to be a prudent, neatly micromanaged business strategy that works well for football club owners. Kaizer Motaung is a well-known trendsetter in football just in the same way Doctor Khumalo has been known in fashion circles. Doctor Khumalo has also been known to have an eye and appetite for very nice luxury cars.

Khumalo had just signed a lucrative offer from Columbus Crew in the Major League Soccer in the United States.

He had been in camp with Bafana Bafana in preparations for the Four Nations Cup.Two tall guys rocked up at the hotel at which Khumalo & Co camped. A receptionist called Doctor Khumalo from his room to reception. This is how Doctor Khumalo relayed the story of his American journey to me.

"Are you Doctor?" An American gentleman asked him with a deep American accent "DAKTA."

Khumalo answered with a yes. A phone call came immediately from Chiefs owner Kaizer Motaung. "Hello Doctor, are you with two American guys there?" Khumalo replied in the affirmative." Please do as I say ok. Kindly sign there next to where I signed. You are going to play in the United States."

Doctor Khumalo signed a two-year contract with the club and was headed for the United States. Doctor Khumalo was one of the 12 designated players in the whole world who would be going to play in the United States' Major League Soccer, amongst them Colombian superstar Carlos Valdaremma and eccentric goalkeeper Jorge Campos from Mexico!

Kaizer Motaung gave Doctor Khumalo all his blessings. Doctor Khumalo broke many supporters' hearts when he announced that he would be leaving Kaizer Chiefs for the United States. In 2010, Doctor Khumalo personally told me that the American deal he was offered was unbelievable and compelling.

"I was a designate player, by far the highest paid player in the team. I was given a big house and a beautiful sports car. They really took care of me. It was really nice in the US."

It is important to give a perspective of Columbus.It is the capital and largest City in the US state of Ohio.Doctor Khumalo had never dreamt of the United States as a career destination. He had been to Los Angeles as a Bafana player in 1993 when they lost 4-0 against a merciless Mexico national team.The defeat would soon make Bafana Bafana become a formidable team that went on to conquer Africa.Mark Fish, one of Doctor's good friends made his debut in the Los Angeles match. The city was named after Christopher Columbus. It was 4th most popolous capital in US behind Phoenix, Arizona and Indianapolis.Columbus Crew is situated there and played in the Ohio Stadium also used by the Buceys Football team at the Ohio State

University. This was not a soccer specific stadium. The soccer specific stadium is called Ohio stadium with a capacity of 102 329 making it the 6th world's biggest stadium ahead of Nou Camp, Estadia do Maracana, Stade de France, Soccer City.The stadium is used as a concert home for U2, Rolling Stones and Mettalica all having played there. It is a picturesque with a cost of over 1.34 million USD.So when Doctor Khumalo left for the United States, there was a lot of reaction to his departure. Many supporters did not take kindly to the news that Doctor Khumalo would be playing elsewhere in the new season. More like in 2018 when Siphiwe Tshabalala left Kaizer Chiefs for a Turkish club. Even worse when Itumeleng Khune almost left Kaizer Chiefs in 2015. However, some held a different view though. Doctor Khumalo had won almost every accolade locally and deserved to go overseas. When Siphiwe Tshabalala left Amakhosi at the age of 33 years, to ply his trade in Turkey, many people were hurt, very hurt that he was leaving Kaizer Chiefs. But many were excited that Tshabalala deserved to showcase his talent to the world in Europe. Many pundits said the move was actually 10 years late. However, in this case, the general feeling was that Doctor Khumalo deserved to play in Europe rather than in the unknown Major League Soccer. Some people were simply ecstatic that South Africa's most famous sportsman would be raking in US dollars which they saw as a major step in his professional career considering his age. Doctor Khumalo had been to several teams in Europe for trials notably at Aston Villa where he made good friends with Dwight Yorke-the Trinidad and Tobago striker who later formed a devastaing partnership with Andy Cole at Man United in the late 90s. Doctor Khumalo could not sign with Aston Villa for some reason. During that time, it was obvious that a UK work permit would have been an impossibility considering that South Africa had not been re-admitted into the international fold. Regrettably, Khumalo came back to continue with his Kaizer Chiefs career. He continued to get enquiries from Turkey. However, nothing tangible ever materialized in Turkey. A few years later, in 1994, Lucas Radebe and the late Phil Masinga made moves to England. It is reported that President Nelson Mandela had to do a motivational letter to give credence to Radebe's work permit application.

Most fans felt it was in fact overdue, looking at the fact that Doctor Khumalo was not getting any younger. At 28, he should have been in Europe already. Abedi Pele had made it in Europe at the age of 17 while Kalusha Bwalya went to Belgium at age 20. Closer to home in Zimbabwe, Peter Ndlovu had become very popular and joined a Premiership club in his teenage years. These were heavy weights in their respective countries. Doctor Khumalo was in the same league of talent as this trio or even better. Why couldn't he get a team to play for in Europe? That was the question in most people's hearts and minds. He too deserved a break overseas. Even if it's the United States, some argued.

Doctor Khumalo signed a two-year contract with the American outfit. He went to the United States amid much fanfare. It was wild when he landed in the USA. At the Crew, Doctor Khumalo was respected and the fans already loved him before he even landed. The mood had been pregnant for his arrival. People had read and heard about him. His dribbling skills had been talked about in the MLS. His goals at Kaizer Chiefs had become an issue within the American press. A lot was expected of the South African star.

I stand to be corrected, in 1996 or thereabout Doctor Khumalo made history by becoming the first South African professional in history to captain an overseas club.It is a record that South Africans like to forget. A history that the local media seems to overlook. Doctor Khumalo was incredibly appointed captain of the club during the off-season camp. The coach Roy Wergele, in his own words, had never seen such a talented player. The players could not believe what Khumalo did at training. He was a phenomenon they were not ready for.

"I had never dribbled people like that, I earned their respect with all I could do with the ball. The guys couldn't believe what they saw so the coach was impressed and surprisingly appointed me captain during the off season. I am happy that I was probably the first player from this country to captain a foreign club." Doctor Khumalo told me

Doctor Khumalo would then lead the Crew to respectable positions during his stay in Ohio.

"Doctor Kumalo is a superstar in Africa and is the most famous player in South Africa. He is supremely gifted and will change the fortunes of the Crew." the club website read before his arrival.

That would be the beginning for greater things for the 29-year-old midfield kingpin. Coincidentally, his new team wore black and gold-the same colours that Khumalo had been gracing for Amakhosi since his professional debut in 1987.In his first match for the Crew, he impressed with his silky touches.The fact is that Columbus Crew had never had a player of such magnificent pedigree and international stature. He was eccentrically adored in the United States.He would be treated like a King in a foreign land–a country with a dark history which dates back hundreds of years of discrimination especially against Blacks and Hispanics.

In no time, Doctor Khumalo pronounced to his supporters in his Kickoff column that he had been given amongst others a nice apartment in Ohio, and an amazing sports car. He was living his dream-making money in Dollar terms. At Columbus Crew, his coach Roy Wergele gave him the freedom and the space to do what he could do best. Doctor Khumalo expressed himself. To the fullest. And with that freedom, Roy Wergele knew the best technique of getting the best out of Doctor Khumalo.

He would win several Man of the Match awards. He helped with numerous assists to get the East Conference outfit a respectable position in the log. Here, 16v scored quite a number of goals in his first season with the Crew.In the United States, soccer like in Europe is quite direct. Its pure business. There are no stop overs. There are no *tsamaya's* and *shibobos*. Khumalo suprisingly fitted well in that system that he'd soon be well known for his incredible ball skills, intelligent passes and a penchant for amazing long-range goals. When he danced on the ball, many American supporters liked it. But with his age, he had mellowed. He did less antics.

He had already gotten out of the showmanship that characterised much of his game in both Bafana Bafana and Kaizer Chiefs colours. He was a mature player now, no longer the type that played to the gallery. He was now a player that looked for results only. This Doctor Khumalo, back home in South Africa was not the Doctor Khumalo we knew. Our Doctor Khumalo mesmerized fans, opponents and his teammates alike. He was a genius of some sorts. He was a jester on the ball who simply needed very little coaching. This is what people wanted to see. What the masses who religiously converged at the Rand Stadium or FNB week in, week out expected. In America, Doctor Khumalo had changed a great deal. He had grown a little bigger in physical built.

"There is so much sophistication in their diet and their training regime. Everything in the US game is scientific. They have a medical doctor for everything," Doctor Khumalo told me.

Khumalo thrived largely on his passing ability. He also thrived on dribbling skills otherwise he probably would not have made it at professional level. Without that skill, and without speed and balance many players remained regular and ordinary. A great deal of players in the streets of Africa have ball skills but lack the speed and the required balance. They can skin their opponent alive anytime. However, in most cases don't break through to the professional ranks because of lack of stamina, physical structure or lack of other complimentary elements. How different was Doctor Khumalo? He was different beacuse he could pass the ball with amazing accuracy. Mark Williams is our witness. He benefited a great deal from Doctor Khumalo. He could also make intelligent runs into space beacuse he was not the marking type. One thing that i observed about 16V was that when he had no choice but to fight for the ball, he would try too hard. He often ended up in referee's books. He would tackle rough and carelessly. One match that comes to my mind was an international match in which he was red carded for stretching his boot high, endangering his opponent.

It is common knowledge that Doctor Khumalo was never was a good marker. He did not have much of stamina and his pace was a serious concern from his early days until he retired. This is what made Shoes Moshoeu play so many games for South Africa and more years at club level while Doctor Khumalo had already retired. Honestly, Shoes Moshoeu, applied himself much more than Doctor Khumalo. The truth is that Doctor Khumalo relied much more on his superior talent. Siphiwe Tshabalala is another player who works his socks off more like Shoes Moshoeu. Quietly and consistently for Kaizer Chiefs over a decade, until he moved overseas in 2018.

The truth is that while Shoes Moshoeu possesed almost all the attributes that Doctor Khumalo had, the glaring difference between them was pace. Shoes, not the best dribbler in the world, had the much-needed pace and balance. Above that, he possessed unbelievable endurance. Truly speaking, they were almost one player in their game. They used their brains. Shoes Moshoeu was however very useful in the air while Doctor Khumalo never seemed to like fighting for the ball in air, nor did he like tussling for it on the ground. That Shoes Moshoeu would do this with aplomb. In fact, Shoes Moshoeu scored some of the best goals of his career with his head-powerful headers from corner kicks or crosses. Doctor Khumalo would idle around the park waiting for a loose ball or a pass from a teammate. Suddenly, he would out of the blue, create magic-a killer pass! Sometimes, a dummy that would leave supporters, his teammates and opponents, all in awe. Doctor Khumalo had apparently tried boxing as a young boy but the techinque he used on the football pitch was unbelievable. I wonder what we could have witnessed had he continued with boxing. He probably could have surpassed another *Kasi* idol boxing hero Baby Jake Matlala.Doctor's techinque was such that while he was a slow player himself, he would take on defenders with so much grip and control on the ball. Any defender from all shapes and forms. Whether it was Papi Khomane, Frank Amankwah or Uke Ukechuku, Khumalo would think on his feet, he would quickly unleash a trick, perfect it on an opponent and leave the defender for dead, square a pint point long cross for a striker to finish off with a powerful header or kick.Indeed his iconic status with

Kaizer Chiefs and Bafana Bafana transformed into a sustained period of excellence for his American club Columbus Crew.

As Sun Tsu would say "a good commander must be deft, niffty and committed to the course", Doctor Khumalo as captain of the Crew seemed to enjoy the game in the United States much better.

In the United States, the not so impressive crowds loved the ocassional *shibobos* and the *tsamayas*. He would dazzle and dribble, create a magical piece of skill when least expected. The supporters would scream in excitement for more. What made the United States more exciting was that in the MLS, there was no big pressure and one could enjoy their game without wondering what supporters expected. In the MLS, a player worried less about what the people in the streets would be saying the following day. What the media would be saying in their various fora. The MLS was a much better relaxed atmosphere for him than at Kaizer Chiefs where 16 million supporters would be expecting magic week in, week out.

At home in South Africa, it is common course that Doctor Khumalo drove the nicest cars. He wore the nicest designer labels and was incredibly famous. Women liked him. The press sold well with him on their cover pages. Therefore, every step Doctor Khumalo took, both on and off the field, was calculated. In the United States, Doctor Khumalo was relatively relaxed, with no big pressure. He however, had on his shoulders the big responsibility of ambassador. He was a highly paid athlete, also captain of the club. He was a designate player solicited, scouted and bought directly by the Major League Soccer to the United States. This was not a simple thing on him. Expectations were there, inevitably. Together with Carlos Valderamma and Alexi Lalas, Doctor Khumalo was King of the ball in the United States.

(15)

Coaching Kaizer Chiefs

Muhsin Ertugrul is a world class, top tactician by any means. He won Kaizer Chiefs a number of trophies in his first spell at the club. With Ertugrul, Kaizer Chiefs have been African Champions of the now defunct Mandela Cup. Muhsin was unlucky in the league with Chiefs losing crucial games therefore getting too much criticism for that. Fans forget that this was the same Muhsin who had just won the club the prestigious African club of the year award. The criticism was somewhat unfair in the sense that Muhsin's philosophy was youth based. The players he had at the time of this spell were very young players. Players such as Rene' Richards had just come to grips with playing at the highest level. Another thing is that every team goes through a rough patch at some stage. Muhsin Ertugrul had been neglecting Doctor Khumalo on the bench. Ace Khuse had just come back from a successful 10-year football career in Turkey. Khuse had just retired from the game after a handful of matches with Chiefs. He together with Doctor Khumalo was made one of the assistant coaches to Muhsin Ertugrul. Doctor Khumalo however appeared to have been pushed into coaching at the time. Doctor Khumalo's heart, as he had always mentioned on several platforms, was with football administration, preferably marketing.

However, Kaizer Motaung was under tremendous pressure. The club was sinking. Muhsin was succumbing to pressure. Kaizer Motaung had to make a tough decision to have Muhsin step aside for a while while Khumalo and Khuse went on with the job as caretakers. They had taken Kaizer Chiefs to unprecedented heights during their time as players. They had an impeccable reputation as players at this club during their heydays. Donald Ace Khuse was named after another Chiefs hero, Ace Ntsoelengoe. Khuse was a great player, gifted with silky skills and a penchant for beautiful short passes. He was a workaholic of note in midfield. He is one of the most dedicated sportsmen I have ever seen. He is a true professional and lives the game without colourful media articles hogging headlines. Doctor Khumalo and Ace Khuse were appointed on an interim basis to lead the most successful club in South Africa. Doctor Khumalo was only 35 years old. Ace was approaching 40 years old. Most people saw that as a crisis for Chiefs. Motaung is often credited with bringing good coaches to South Africa. Names such as Jeff Butler, Augusto Palacios, Muhsin Ertugrul and Paul Dolezar remind us of the great scouting network Motaung has around the world. This time, Motaung was probably buying time as he wanted more time to go back to his European network of contacts to look for a permanent manager. The media did not spare Ace Khune and Doctor Khumalo. Some called them novices. Some sympathized with the two legends mostly because of their indelible historical contribution to the club. Shoes Moshoeu, Kaizer Motaung Jr and young players such as Tinashe Negomasha, Buti Sithole and Richards would now be looked at seriously. Shoes Moshoeu had come back from overseas where he had starred for Genclerbirligi, Kocaliespor and Fernabache in the Turkish Super League. What struck Amakhosi supporters was that while Shoes had been an intergral part of Bafana Bafana he was not used regularly at Kaizer Chiefs-because of age-but not much was expected of him but something new was expected from the star. Here is a former Fernabache star with many youngsters who were crumbling due to lack of game time. Perhaps the pressure that goes with playing for Chiefs also took a toll on the youngsters. Shoes Moshoeu would play a pivotal role in motivating the younsgsters. Doctor and Ace Khuse, great club legends-on the bench, and with Shoes on the pitch, there was hope that the youngsters would feel obliged to pull up their socks. And suddenly they did! Chiefs dramatically re-grouped and won a few games under the leadership of what the media had nicknamed the two DK's- Donaldo Khuse and Doctor Khumalo. Shoes Moshoeu was getting more game time scoring important goals in important matches. I attended many of these matches. I remember one match in Newlands in Cape Town against Engen Santos. It was a thriller. That day, I saw the real Shoes Moshoeu. He reignited my memories of his scintillating form in the Afcon 1996. Arthur Zwane too, he was amazing. It was telepathy in the true meaning of the word. They salvaged the Kaizer Chiefs heritage, history and reputation that day. They totally, completely saved the club.

Kaizer Chiefs finished the season in a respectable position and the following season the two caretakers were replaced by Ernst Middendorp from Germany.The German-born mentor brought his own technical team to the club. It now like looked Doctor Khumalo would finally get his old dream of going into club administration.

Khumalo was however deployed to youth ranks Under 17 team! His real coaching career started here. Here, he impressed a great deal with the club youth team.

"It might sound like a demotion but it's actually a bigger responsibility of being part of the development of young players and will surely pay devidents in the long run."

Khumalo appeared to be unfaced by what the media felt was a demotion. He actually sounded all too happy to have been relieved off the stress of leading the senior Amakhosi team.

"Obviously it's a challenge as I have never worked in developing youngsters before, the exciting part about this is that it offers room for personal growth as a coach," Khumalo told club website.

Khumalo seems to have an eye for talent. When Pirates introduced Mbulelo Oldjohn Mabizela to professional football, Khumalo was one of the first

people to talk highly of the player. Oldjohn went on to play for Bafana Bafana and Tottenham Hotspurs in the English Premier League. Doctor Khumalo also raved and raved highly about a young Itumeleng Khune the moment the player was promoted to the senior team. Khune has since grown into one of the finest goalkeepers in the world. Khune's distribution ability is ranked amongst the best three in world football.

Khumalo continued to coach the Chiefs Under 15-17 teams. He seemed happy with the team's progress. I had an opportunity to talk to Doctor Khumalo about his development duties.

"I have always said development is the way to go. I think Chiefs are doing something good. But it will take time. I'm happy with the progress the youngsters are making. Its very encouraging. It's a real eye opener for me."

Khumalo said he would be happy if all sports teams emphasized on development. Khumalo lamented on the results of the South African Olympique team that salvaged only one medal by Khotso Mokoena.

"I think we should look at our development holistically. If you look at Americans, they spend a lot and time monitoring progress. They narture talent and make it the best in the world. They put in not only money but serious effort too. Jamaica is also doing well in that regard hence they win a lot of medals at world competitions."

A few years later, Kaizer Chiefs changed coaches from Middendorp to Vladimir Vermezovic who was also replaced after average achievements with the team. Enter Stuart Baxter, an Englishman who had coached Bafana Bafana with less than satisfactory record before. Baxter had not been given a truly fair chance by SAFA then, but proved to be Motaung's saviour when he led Chiefs in his second spell in South Africa. He won two league trophies in the three seasons he was with Chiefs. Baxter left for Turkey after some disagreement with club management about the direction the club was taking. Turkey did not work out. Stuart Baxter only lasted for two months in Turkey before landing another spell with Supersport United. He took Supersport United from the doldrums of relegation fears to a respectable position in the league. At Supersport, Baxter signed up many of his stars of the successful Kaizer Chiefs side he coached the year before. Stuart Baxter was lured by SAFA from his lucrative Supersport United job to Bafana Bafana. Baxter is now in his second spell with Bafana Bafana. During the successful Kaizer Chiefs period, Baxter had Doctor Khumalo as his Assistant. Together, they won really big. Big things. Many people are still calling for that partnership as Kaizer Chiefs negotiates its way back to the top of the South African football ladder. Under Baxter and Doctor Khumalo, Amakhosi played very good football. Their philosphy was based on extraordinary transitional attack which often caught opposition in sleep. This Kaizer Chiefs team flowed. And they worked like an oiled machine. The players spoke highly of Baxter and his assistant Doctor Khumalo. Baxter was an extremely good manager and a shrewd tactician whose strength lied in precision, research and meticulous preparation for matches. In my over 26 years of following Kaizer Chiefs, I have never personally seen a better coach than Stuart Baxter at Naturena. Even the revered Ted Dumitru was not as compelling as Baxter. Baxter was a great manager who brought supporters back to the stadium. His decisions were well thought out. Players such as Morgan Gould, Reneilwe Letsholonyane, Siphiwe Tshabalala and Tshepo Masilela excelled under him. Doctor Khumalo the assistant coach, seemed to grow in leaps and bounds with occasional catertaker responsibilities. When Baxter did not travel to Ivory Coast for Kaizer Chiefs' Confederations Cup fixture, Doctor Khumalo took charge. When Baxter was suspended against AmaTuks in a league match, Doctor Khumalo held the fort quite decently. Doctor Khumalo was elated when Baxter was re-appointed Bafana Bafana coach in May 2017 replacing Shakes Mashaba who was fired for making what SAFA deemed as unpalatable comments reportedly made live on television. Doctor Khumalo congratulated SAFA for choosing the best coach available saying that Baxter was the best choice if SAFA 'truly looked into the future.' He emphasized Baxter's ability to lay a foundation on which SAFA would be able to tap even after his tenure. Doctor Khumalo told Soccer Laduma that he learnt a great deal under Baxter. He said that he would be happy to see SAFA giving Baxter necessary assistance. Khumalo called for necessary patience to allow Baxter to build a formidable national team which could possibly unite the nation again and qualify for big continental tournaments.

(16)

The State v Doctor Khumalo

Saturday 6 April 2008, South Africa woke up to news that Doctor Khumalo had been admitted into Flora Clinic in Johannesburg after crashing his black BMW Z4. The incident happened at around 5am that fateful Sunday. When Etv broke the news later that evening, the news had already reached far flung areas like Botswana and Cape Town where i was at the time of the accident. I first got the news from friends around Cape Town. Ace Mogomotsi, a prominent Public Relations practioner in Botswana called me all the way from Gaborone asking if indeed Doctor Khumalo had been involved in a car accident! Only I could know, according to Ace Orapeleng!

The papers had a field day the following Monday. The Sowetan newspaper put Doctor Khumalo on the front page. It was expected afterall. In terms of popularity in South Africa, Nelson Mandela aside, the number two spot is still undecided, I think even to this day. Doctor Khumalo is certainly amongst the contenders. He certainly competes with the likes of Archbishop Tutu, Julius Malema, Winnie Madikizela-Mandela, Jacob Zuma and the likes of Cassper Nyovest', Trevor Noah and Bonang Matheba. So, it was expected that the press would sensationalise the story to sell big time and big news. Cape Town community papers also wrote extensively about the accident. I switched on Cape Talk radio, then i switched to 702 Radio, and Radio 2000. It was Doctor Khumalo! On Metro FM, listeners called throughout the various shows interrupting the scheduled topics. It appeared that people were disappointed but a great deal of them sympathized with their hero. It was a rather subdued moment for most of us. It was a devastating moment. The news was not really coming out as sharp and clear as one would have expected. The stories were confusing. But to some of us, what was more important was that Doctor Khumalo was alive. That was a huge relief.

This was the second accident in four years for Doctor Khumalo! Doctor had experienced another accident while coming from Lucas Radebe's wedding in Mafikeng in the North West a few years prior. However, the headlines then were not as magnified and sensationalised as the Maraisburg scene. But what really happened? Suprisingly, media houses speculated on drunken driving. I could not believe it. Doctor Khumalo has had an impeccable career without blemishes of ill discipline. I had never known or heard of him as someone who imbibed in alcoholic beverages. If he did, I assumed he was very careful and highly professional about it. I may have simply assumed because most of the soccer stars of his day, disappeared from the game due to alcohol. Doctor Khumalo spent almost 20 years playing the game, under tremendous expectations from his fans, supporters, coaches, teammates, family and the media. A lot of pressure from Kaizer Chiefs. A great deal of pressure from Kaizer Motaung himself who had brought up the young Doctor Khumalo under his wing as his own son who played with both the late Thabo Motaung and Bobby Motaung-Kaizer's eldest sons. Doctor Khumalo could not crumble now. Never. I refused to agree with those who said Doctor Khumalo had been drunk. I preferred to wait for the principle of *Audi Alteram Partem* to apply in the courts of law. I told myself to wait for his side of story-because for every story, there are three sides. Your story, his story and the truth.

"Khumalo's German sedan had collided with a taxi carrying 3 passengers, one of them a pregnant woman! It is believed that the pregnant woman suffered serious injuries."

Doctor Khumalo and his female passenger were taken to Flora Clinic on the West Rand. This was confirmed by Johanesburg Metro Police spokesperson Inspector Edna Mamonyane. Inspector Mamonyane would then tell Sowetan that investigations would determine whether Doctor Khumalo had been over speeding or not. Drunk or not!

What made this accident a month-long issue is that a few weeks prior to the accident, Mamelodi Sundowns speedy winger Lorato Chabangu had appeared in court on charges of drunken driving. Chabangu had had another charge before of similar fashion but was let go on a technicality. Another great South African cricketer of global standards, Herschelle Gibbs had made headlines in February in an alcohol related incident which occured in Sea Point in Cape Town.

Another star, a largely popular music superstar Mandoza now late, had earlier been involved in an accident in which two people perished in Roodeport. The Kwaito kingpin had just attended an awards ceremony in Sun City in Pilanesburg when the accident happened. Repeated calls were made from many quarters of the media for National Prosecuting Authority (NPA) to come out with a case against Khumalo. Doctor Khumalo then set the record straight in an interview with Drum magazine! He was flanked by his beautiful wife Blanche Garises. Blanche looked quite disturbed in the magazine. She looked quite uneasy on the cover of the magazine. Doctor Khumalo was calm and collected. This was nothing to him, it appeared. After all, Doctor Khumalo had already experienced a great deal before in his pressure-filled life. That life. The main bone of contention besides his alledged drunken status was, who Doctor Khumalo was with in that BMW Z4 when the German sports car crashed onto the mini combi? Boom! Doctor Khumalo was with one Lizzy Moloto! The press wrote so. But who is Lizzy Moloto? Where were they coming from? Going where?

Doctor Khumalo denied the allegations made in the media about his state at the time of the accident. He further flatly denied knowing Lizzy Moloto. The super fly beauty queen came out spewing all sorts of vitriol about the much-publicized incident.

Sunday Sun reported that Lizzy Moloto had been" seriously hurt by accusations."

Lizzy Moloto had a few years ago, been a Sunbabe in the same publication. However, later, Doctor Khumalo in his Drum interview, would not deny ever meeting or being with Lizzy Moloto but stressed that they had not met during the day on which Doctor Khumalo was MC at a church congregation in Potchefstroom.

"We chatted and when it was time to leave, i decided to go with somebody as it was already late at the time." Lizzy was firm and unapologetic

"I dont know him and i have never been with him. I only know Doctor Khumalo from TV and magazines. To top it, he's not even my type. I am happy where i am right now. My dignity is at stake and I will not rest until this matter is cleared." Lizzy told The Sunday Sun.

This statement shocked some people. I was personally puzzled as to what Lizzy meant when she said Doctor Khumalo was not her type! And that she "would not rest until the matter is cleared."I still think Lizzy was trying to steal the show. Doctor Khumalo is obviously not perfect like any other human being. But i do not think it warranted Lizzy Moloto the right to sound like that. Doctor Khumalo was in fact in a relatively new marriage with Blanche Garises. The couple was busy focusing on their future and respective careers. However, this was too far from the scenario of Rebecca Loose who once told the world that she had been busy with English football idol David Beckham, prompting Victoria Beckham to spend more time with Hip Hop mogul Damon Dash.

In 2016, Doctor Khumalo's wife Blanche Garises announced in a newspaper that she had filed for divorce from Doctor Khumalo! I can not pretend that I knew the couple by any stretch. But I had worked briefly with them when I booked them to visit Botswana. They were cool, quite nice, excited. They even visited my home village, Mochudi. They met my family and my son Rene'. We took pictures. It was an unbelievable experience. Together, we did some charity work for Bakgatla-Boloka-Matshelo; an NGO which looks after people afflicted by

HIV/AIDS in my village. The couple donated a few goodies to the orphans. Above that, their presence inspired the kids quite considerably. It was a beautiful gesture, a memorable visit. The community was delighted to see their TV star in the village. Now, the news of the divorce shocked many people including my two aunts Mabel and Joice who truly loved the couple's humility during their visit to Mochudi. The couple had been married for nearly 10 years when they divorced. Their wedding was extra ordinarily covered by the media. It was shown on TV show Top Billing in South Africa. Blanche' Garises is a former beauty queen. She had previously won Miss Namibia. Blanche is a tall, stunning woman of mixed heritage. She is a Nama of German descent, she told me. A super beautiful woman by any standards. The media, as expected wrote extensively about this divorce. Doctor Khumalo conceeded in the Sunday World newspaper that the marriage had broken down irretrievably and would not go further in detail. Newspapers which took interest in the divorce speculated that the divorce would set Doctor Khumalo off an amount between R8 million to R12 million! The couple have a handsome young boy named Diego. Little Diego is obviously named after one of Doctor Khumalo's favourite football stars,Diego Maradona. According to Doctor Khumalo, in an interview with Drum Magazine in 2018, Diego Khumalo is a promising soccer player today. Doctor Khumalo however stressed that Diego's studies, not football-are a priority for now.

Doctor Khumalo has always been very private about his love life. Throughout his life newspapers could only speculate on who Doctor Khumalo was dating. From musicians to top TV presenters and beauty queens. The speculation continued until he married Blanche Garises. And even now after their divorce, the speculation continues. By the Grand Palm hotel poolside, Lawrence Ookeditse cheekly asked Doctor Khumalo, if indeed he has ever dated the all powerful and beautiful Jessica Motaung! Doctor Khumalo was non-commital, and replied "but why do people think so?" That was as far as Doctor Khumalo could go. Jessica Motaung is a former beauty queen who went all the way to win Miss World 1st Princess prize in the late 90's. She is Kaizer Motaung's most prominent daughter who also works at the club as a Marketing Director. I always took it as an assumption that people linked Doctor Khumalo to Jessica Motaung because they grew up and worked together at Kaizer Chiefs. The duo also both graced social events for many years because of their attractive looks and high social status.

My overall observation was that Doctor Khumalo is generally a shy and private person. Not much like the late Shoes Moshoeu. But Doctor Khumalo actually prefers his love life to remain private. Before he married Blanche Garises, Doctor Khumalo had reportedly dated the beautiful Melanie Son for quite sometime. Melanie has been married to music genius Zwai Bala until recently. Quite beautiful, also of mixed descent, Melanie Son is a celebrated television and radio presenter who prefers to be quiet despite her high social stature. Their long-time romance was widely reported in the media but with little coming from both to confirm or deny the rumors. However, the Sunday World recently linked Doctor Khumalo to a beautiful Pretoria businesswoman Tshwanelo Ntshudisane who reportedly dabbles in property development and corporate communications. The two have remained quiet about their alledged romance. As I have stated, for me it is only normal that many people would want to dig deeper into what Doctor Khumalo does in his private space. As much as he wishes to remain a private person, this remains an illusion because he opened his life to the public when Ted Dumitru gave him that successful debut in 1987. This book is obviously not about trivialities around the love life of Doctor Khumalo. It seeks to be an articulation of Doctor Khumalo's illustrious football career from a fan's perspective. It further seeks to cement his legacy for the future. To chronicle his journey through a fan's perspective. But let us accept that Doctor Khumalo's love life remains a substantial subject of interest to many people. Just as much as his soccer skills have been a consumption by many in the 17 years of his professional soccer career as a player, his private life has also been of interest to people in general. Both interested in football and those not really interested in football,like my two aunts.

But the truth is that Doctor Khumalo's name, just like Jacob Zuma, Julius Malema, Hlaudi Motsoeneng, Bishop Tutu or Bonang Matheba sells really big in the media. People have taken keen interest in these people's lives. Whether the news is good news or bad news. The difference is the same. The paper flies off the shelves. And very fast. For the media to increase sales, they need something spectacular or at least some negativity to report on. Doctor Khumalo has been a victim of this too. However, Doctor Khumalo has been fairly fortunate in his life. A lot of more good things has been written about him compared to the bad. Doctor Khumalo, perhaps inexplicably, has without doubt really been the media's best and favorite son. His relationship with both Soccer Laduma and Kickoff magazine, South Africa's biggest soccer publications is quite durable. This relationship, particularly with Soccer Laduma, grows everyday as evidenced by the column Doctor Khumalo writes for this publication for well over 15 years now!

(17)

Life in Retirement

Percy Adams is quite a flamboyant guy. Adams is a shrewd go-getter, a highly polished and skilled negotiator well known within corporate circles in Johannesburg. He boasts a massive contact network and an astonishing marketing acumen. Percy Adams looked after Doctor Khumalo's business interests for many years. The business manager-cum-confidante is described by the media as the man behind Doctor Khumalo's business affairs. Adams had this to say in 2000 in an interview with the now defunct Sportslife magazine. The discussion was centred on the future of his long-time client and friend Doctor Khumalo. At the time, Doctor Khumalo was already showing signs of fatigue at the top level.

"We are busy preparing for his retirement. We intend buying a stake in Kaizer Chiefs. That's why we are giving him managerial training. We have already provided him with a valuable reading material to prepare him for that role. We will be spending R500, 000,00 and in a year or two he should be ready," Adams said.

"We would like to organize a website for him, and we are hoping to launch it early in the new year. What we don't want is Doctor being just a front man. He must be a hands on guy who will actually be clinching the deals. We also want Shoes Moshoeu to get involved. We already have offices in Sandton and Doctor is very excited. He can't wait to get started. Its time to say bye bye to the beautiful game that's done so much for him."

Doctor Khumalo seems smart with numbers. He is doing fairly well in business. When I hosted Doctor Khumalo in Botswana, he was cagey about his reported various income streams except to say that Puma and other sponsors looked after him quite well. He also mentioned to me that he was exploring mining opportunities in Africa. Beyond that, what I know is that Doctor Khumalo remains a largely sought-after public speaker and an enormous brand ambassador. He does coaching clinics and product activations for the various brands he represents. In doing all these, he charges a fortune. He does not come cheap. He is also very diligent about what he involves his brand and name in. He is also quite sensitive about where he takes his brand. For example, when I finally contacted him for the event I needed him to grace in Botswana in 2010, his first response was.

"How big are your airplanes?"

Coming from Botswana, it was rather a kick in my teeth. Air Botswana is not Emirates or Singapore Airlines. We are certainly not playing with the big boys such as Qatar Airways,Ethiopian Airways, SAA or British Airways. Air Botswana is a small airline. This is despite the fact that Botswana remains the world's biggest producer of diamonds by both value and volume. Botswana is also the second biggest producer of beef in the world. I expect the Botswana government to do more in this regard because this could very well be the question that Lionel Messi or Samuel Eto'o could ask if and when they needed to visit Botswana. It could be any business person wanting to visit. I picked up that Doctor Khumalo looked after his brand quite well. He jealously guards it for it is his biggest asset in retirement. His brand is his asset for the rest of his life in the same way that Pele, Jomo Sono, Diego Maradona or David Beckham have managed to live off their names and brands. These names have been turned into massive brands. These brands bring them money. When Doctor Khumalo arrived in Botswana, we had booked him one of the 4-star hotels in the country. After the press conference, a day later, Doctor Khumalo called me aside and asked whether there was no better hotel in the city! MacLean Letshwiti, the current BFA President who is also a vastly successful businessman in Botswana, moved Doctor Khumalo and his wife Blanche and their assistant Leandra Ribberts to the more affluent Grand Palm Hotel. The request to move to Grand Palm was a simple demonstration of just how much Doctor Khumalo looked after his brand. During the two-day tour, we chauffered Doctor Khumalo and his team in a brand-new Mercedes Benz supplied by Avis Botswana whose Executive Chairman is MacLean Letshwiti. I learnt a few things about etiquette and hospitality during that tour. Here, I learnt a great deal about brand management. Consequently, I decided to take a course on Brand Management with the University of Cape Town specifically on how to manage sports people and brands. This, I hope will go a long way.

In August 2017, Doctor Khumalo announced that he would be joining Baroka FC as a Technical Director concurrently working as Head of Marketing. Baroka FC are owned by Khurishi Mphahlele, a Limpopo businessman who has outlined a R150 million vision to build Baroka FC a state-of-the-art facility in the mould of Kaizer Chiefs Naturena home. Baroka FC are quite ambitious. The rumors leading to the envisaged announcement did not bother me. Doctor Khumalo is a well-known city guy who had never really lived outside Johannesburg except for his stint in Argentina and another in Ohio, in the United States. He had tried a sleepy Benois Aires in Argentina for 6 months and came back. He had lived in an insular Ohio in the United States for nearly two years and came back. Would he relocate to Limpopo? On press conference day, high flying, respected businessman and super agent Jazzman Mahlakgane was in the picture. Doctor Khumalo broke the news!

"I hereby confirm that I have parted ways with Chiefs and the Chairman has given me his blessings to grow my brand."

"I wish to announce that I will be taking a new role as Technical Director of Baroka FC. I look forward to a new journey."

The banners at the press conference where that of Mahlakgane's management agency, Professionalz Marketing and Management. I knew then that this was serious business. Big money. Big vision. Big brands. Jazzman Mahlakgane manages top personalities like Teko Modise and Siphiwe Tshabalala. He also managed Itumeleng Khune for a long time. When Mahlakgane comes into the picture, it gets very serious. The popular Beachwood Hotel is a true example of his transformation prowess.

"Jazzman looks after the Doctor Khumalo brand, the plan is to take it into a new direction as it evolves," Doctor Khumalo told Robert Marawa on his tv show.

My confidence in this new venture grew exponentially when I saw Jazzman Mahlakgane in the Baroka deal. I could tell this was a vision unfolding. Doctor Khumalo wants to contribute in a larger, more involved scale in football. Doctor Khumalo had been with Kaizer Chiefs since 1985. Doctor Khumalo was now given the blessings by Kaizer Motaung to grow elsewhere. However, Kaizer Motaung was quick to mention that Doctor Khumalo would be allowed back at Naturena anytime should the Baroka venture not pen out good.

"His last words, after everything was said and done, that "its time for you to grow. But in everything you do, remember that you are representing me and Kaizer Chiefs," Doctor Khumalo said about Kaizer Motaung.

The move,it appears-was caused not only by Doctor Khumalo's desire to test new waters but a failed attempt to get his own proposal accepted by Kaizer Chiefs. This proposal was about yet exciting opportunities presented by Doctor Khumalo in relation to his brand. This included television and media work he continues to do which remunerates him handsomely. In the end though, Doctor Khumalo left Kaizer Chiefs in an unprecedented move that shocked many. However, as it is always with Doctor Khumalo fans and supporters, they also somewhat appeared to agree with this move, although reluctantly. The general feeling was that eventually

Doctor Khumalo would be able to do something away from the club he has so been loyal to all his life. This is the club that gave him everything but two personal wishes; shareholding and a permanent coaching job!

Just after Baroka deal, Doctor Khumalo was announced as brand ambassador for Ford!

'Doc Khumalo, one of the best-known names on the South African soccer scene, has been appointed a brand ambassador for Ford, and will be proudly driving a Ford Mustang for the next 12 months,' the statement read.

'Doc Khumalo is a legendary South African football player, and we are delighted to have him sign up as a brand ambassador for Ford and driving our legendary Mustang,' said Neale Hill, director marketing, sales and service, Ford Motor Company Sub-Saharan Africa (SSA) region.

Doctor Khumalo is now turning heads behind the wheel of a Ford Mustang GT Cabriolet, which is powered by the mighty 306kW 5.0-litre V8 engine – thus further raising the profile of one of the world's most iconic automotive nameplates. This is one of South Africa's top-selling sports car ranges. Ford Mustang is one of the fastest cars in the world.

Doctor Khumalo was humble about this great opportunity with Ford. Like the diplomat he has always been, he was motivational in his acceptance speech.

'I am more than delighted to be part of the Ford family,' said Doc Khumalo.

'Driving in the Ford Mustang GT 5.0 will not only be inspirational to me but also to those around me,'Khumalo said.

A few months later, Doctor Khumalo appeared in Sportpesa regalia! He is now the brand ambassador of this massive Pan-African brand which has also taken European football by storm. These are the big brands which clearly demonstrate the mass commercial appeal the Doctor Khumalo brand attracts. His life in retirement is clearly well taken care of by the solid support system brought about by his big name. This big name and big brand were a result of his splendid performances during his heyday as a soccer player. In the winter of 2018, Doctor Khumalo parted ways with Baroka FC following a mutual agreement with the club. The club disclosed that they could no longer sustain the relationship due to financial constraints. The response Doctor Khumalo gave the media suggested that both parties parted ways amicably and that the club was very happy with the contribution he had made at the club.

(18)

Music & Film

Doctor Khumalo became the first professional soccer player in South Africa to get into music. He recorded an album in the early 90's with popular Dj Bob Mabena. Mabena is now a respected radio executive in South Africa. Doctor Khumalo is very,very close to Bob Mabena. The pair quickly decided on an album. This propelled Doctor Khumalo's popularity to sky levels. He was the man on the mike, the King on the field. This is what Bob Mabena had to say about their music album.

"The match up with Doc Khumalo under Mdu Masilela and Lindelani Mkhize was a blast. Record sales were not even part of our agenda. It was about hanging out with different people from different backgrounds and performing, sometimes at the most bizarre of venues."

Doctor Khumalo continued with his singing when he teamed up with Sbu in an album in 2004.He has however remained very cagey about his general music plans. In 2017, Doctor Khumalo appeared in the video of Oskido's Amagrootman, a musical piece which sought to give respect to the legends in the industry. Oskido is a mercurial music genius with so much influence on the South African music business. In this video, the revered DJ Fresh also makes a grand appearance as a legend. This video, is unbelievable. Great music brands teaming up, *amagrootmen* converging with soccer grootman Doctor Khumalo! Respect! Respect! Respect!

"A few guys have tried it. I just felt I should do it with Bob and I am still happy with my soccer but when I do get an opportunity, I will always do it because I love music," Doctor Khumalo said on his hit with Bob Mabena.

Footballers have not been great music stars when they try to dabble in that field. Ghanaian top striker Asamoah Gyan is a musician when he is not playing. Gyan has not reached the success in music that can be compared to what he has achieved on the field of play. Several musicians continue to work with Gyan on collaborations. The other

player who has done music is Benni McCarthy. Good music. The former Porto FC striker is a rare example of a very successful footballer who played in the musical world. But Benni McCarthy's case was an exception. He was featured in TkZee's album which did extremely well. TkZee was a great Kwaito group at the time, resonating with middle class urban groups from the townships of South Africa. The album did extremely well and the group's members went on to become hugely successful individual stars. McCarthy is yet to do his own album. Jabu Pule has also tried to dabble in music but with very little success. He has since gone back to analyzing matches on television in his retirement.

In 2010, Doctor Khumalo featured in a German South African production which produced a breathtaking and insightful movie titled Themba. He was alongside the beautiful Afro-Soul genius Simphiwe Dana and former Arsenal goalkeeper Jens Lehmann. The movie sought to relay a message of triumph over adversity. A truly inspirational African story wherein a young boy Themba beat all odds to realise his dream of playing for his country. This is despite his painful story of HIV/AIDS, poverty and violence all of which had plagued him and his family. Doctor Khumalo played himself as a coach of the South Africa U-21 team for which Themba played. Except for Doctor Khumalo, we have not had any other footballer in South Africa in an international film production. Doctor Khumalo has truly been loved by the world. He has also made a few appearances in South Africa's biggest, much celebrated popular local television soapie, Generations.

Epilogue

As you will have seen, this book was written conversational style; it is primarily a football fan's perspective. I have obviously drawn from historical material compiled by myself and others in both the sporting and social fronts. For me, Doctor Khumalo encapsulates all that which is great and beautiful about football. It is somehow, somewhat no surprise that Doctor Khumalo is still very popular to this day. The story of his discovery is also quite interesting. I have enjoyed doing research for this book, travelling around and enquiring. I believe I have done a faily good but modest research on the product. It has been humbling to recognize the universal admiration for Doctor Khumalo.I do not recall any glaring negativity about Doctor Khumalo. This is quite unique with celebrities and stars of his stature, of his fame and fortune. My greatest regret though is that, I was never able to meet Doctor Khumalo's father Eliakim Pro Khumalo for he passed on a long time ago. I was also unable to meet Doctor Khumalo's mother *mama* Mable Khumalo. But to *mama* Khumalo and *ntate* Pro, we must be eternally grateful to them for bequeathing us this great talent named Doctor Khumalo. I was also unable to meet Doctor Khumalo's only sister and sibling Fikile due to constraints beyond me. Also, palpably missing in this tribute, is the esteemed Kaizer Motaung whom I had initially wished to meet but failed due to bureaucracy and also the shape the book took in the end. As you will notice, there is no foreword in this tribute. Only Kaizer Motaung could do the foreword on Doctor Khumalo. Unfortunately, I was constrained by many factors. So, to *ntate* Kaizer Motaung, the undisputed father of South Africa football as Dr Patrice Motsepe calls Kaizer Motaung-South Africa and the world are plentifully thankful to you for giving a young Doctor Khumalo a massive platform on which he majestically marched, mesmerizing the world. Doctor Khumalo used this international stage to inspire millions of youngsters in the townships. From Soweto to Langa, Galeshewe to Seshego, Old Naledi in

Botswana to Katutura in Namibia and elsewhere in Africa.It would have been nicer if i had met Doctor Khumalo's role model Ace Ntsoelengoe.Unfortunately, Ace Ntsoelengoe passed on while the book was still a peripheral idea. It would have been interesting to get unfetted access to Doctor Khumalo's Bafana Bafana teammates of the 1996 Afcon squad. I missed out on the late Mguyo Samuel Temane and the energetic Freedie Sadaam Maake who have been unbelievable supporters of Doctor Khumalo the player and Doctor Khumalo the legend and Doctor Khumalo the brand. The duo has religiously supported Kaizer Chiefs. They have been there since day one of Doctor Khumalo's career. But this being an unauthorized biography, there was a great deal of contraints around legalities and access. Therefore, this book is first and foremost, predominantly and fundamentally, my view of the legend as a soccer fan. It is my perspective as Doctor Khumalo's biggest fan in the whole world. It just had to be done. With or without Doctor Khumalo, I had to do it my own way for future generations and for the world. For any mistakes in the book especially around facts and content, I take full responsibility in advance. To those who may not be pleased by the book and the content– whilst I must apologize in advance–I must equally confess that I actually find solace in the fact that even in our genuine celebration of our heroes and heroines, we still remain fallible as human beings.

Reference & Bibligraphy

Kickoff, Kaizer Chiefs website, The Sowetan, The Sunday Times, City Press, Soccer Laduma, Soccer News, Sports Life, PSL website, SAFA website, MLS website, Google, Drum Magazine, The Citizen, Columbus Crew website, Cape Times, Mzanzi magic by Joe Letakgomo, Madiba's Boys, Man of Action by Roger de Sa, AFRICA UNITED,The Art of War by Sun Tsu, The Big FIX; How South Africa Stole The 2010 World Cup, The Curse of Teko Modise, Soccer Laduma, Doctor Khumalo Soccer Laduma Columns, Doctor Khumalo Kickoff series, Coach; The Life and Soccer Times of Clive Barker, The JoburgPost. The Sunday Sun, Sunday World.

Acknowledgements

This work is a synergistic product of many minds. Writing this book, I relied on the hospitality, advice, expertise, patience, love and generosity of many people. In no particular order, I wish to thank them. To Kgosikgolo Kgafela Kgafela II of Bakgatla-ba-Kgafela, your autobiographical testimony in the King's Journal played a significant role in resuscitating the idea of this publication. Your story of optimism over adversity reignited my desire to publish this tribute. Thank you Kgosikgolo. Former President Thabo Mbeki is in my world-one of the finest writers i know. His writings have generally been a compelling inspiration for me, so thank you Zizi. My late grandmother Mosele Sikwane, to whom I have dedicated this book, was a monumental pillar in what I have since become as a person all round. I say thank you, posthumously. I want to thank my own mother Mmabodisa Matlapeng for she has always believed that all my dreams are valid. She has not only put me through school but she's still teaching me so much to this day. She has taught me the power of optimism over gloom. To my father Segale Matlapeng, your love for Doctor Khumalo has had an organic and profound ripple-effect on me. The consequence thereof is this book, so thank you so much. The beautiful Eunice Maswabi has truly been a phenomenal gift of life. She has been a consummate and quintessential friend throughout time, and forever I trust. She has really pushed me to complete this book. Thank you. Thank you to *malome* Shoti Sikwane. You mean everything to me. If it were not for you, i would probably not have paid attention to soccer at all. My son Rene' looks up to me, I draw inexplicable strength from seeing his expectant eyes, so thank you. Honorable Dithapelo Keorapetse has been my best friend since the age of 14 years! He is the biggest supporter and fan of my dreams. He is the most honest, most patient yet optimistic person I have ever met. Honorable Dithapelo has always believed in my dreams. He has been behind the protracted dream to publish this book, so thank you. I thank all my four sisters Onalenna,

Kelebogile, Seeletso and Larona Matlapeng who have been a catalytic sensation that propelled me everyday. To my younger brother Bogatsu Matlapeng who looks up to me as the best writer in the world, I say thank you. I owe particular gratitude to my beautiful and very patient aunts Mabel Tshutlhedi and Joyce Sikwane including my cousin Gorata Sikwane who are big Doctor Khumalo fans. I am grateful to *rangwane* Seabe Ramphaleng for you bought me all the soccer publications when I could not afford any as a small boy. Thank you to my closest cousin-cum-confidante Balosang Jonathan Sikwane. You are a durable, true brother indeed. To my good cousin Malebogo Selemogo, thank you for being a phenomenal woman in many aspects of my life. To my pleasant cousin Kokie Phalaagae, God bless you for the support. My good cousin,an equally gifted writer Dikatso Selemogwe, thank you for being a good motivation in my writing journey. Remember where we come from? *Abuti* Disang Selemogwe has also been a great colleague in sport, a good brother. My good cousin-cum-consultant-in literature Kealeboga Seitlhomolo, thanks for the support over the years. Thank you to my kind cousin Nako Mogale. You have been amazing as an English specialist pro-bono. *Abuti* Johnny Tshutlhedi and Ben Moilwa have been great brothers completely, buying me soccer books as a young boy, so thank you. My cousin Molatlhegi Nare with whom i played ball, and with whom I grew up,thank you. I must thank Segobye Bokole, my football coach as a youngster. I appreciate the many sacrifices including this book that my brother Rasthoem Simons has made in my life generally. Simons will forever grace my heart. So, thank you. Thank you to *Attorney* Sivuyile Jama who throughout law school was a true comrade. Jama always believed that i would ultimately realize my dream. Thanks to my very good friends *Attorney* Kago Theo Pelekekae, *Attorney* Tebogo Balesamang and Kagiso Nnoi-a good man. Remember the sleepless nights we spent together sharing and discussing this 'monumental dream' at Liberty residence of UWC? Khali Mothopeng is a fantastic Kaizer Chiefs supporter, an important friend in my life, thank you for the long time support. Thank you to Enock Kedisitse-a true compatriot and a soccer man through and through. Thank you Lucas Modimana, a long-time friend from Primary School-a great intellectual fountain from whom I draw a great deal. Thank you Joel Kgodungwe, Lame Bokole and Onkabetse

Keofitlhile-great soccer friends from Primary School.Journalists are generally not a sharing breed,so i am grateful to the talented group of colleagues at 365 Digital Anthony McLennan, Lascius Ncube, Armien Harris, Khaya Ndubane, Thapelo Moloantoa and Trevor Kramer. I must plentifully thank Anthony McLennan who like Mqondisi Dube,polished and refined my writing skills. May God bless these guys. Throughout research and writing of this book, I relied on Anthony McLennan's invaluable advice, rapid response and wide contact network. Thank you to The founder of The Mirror newspaper Moeti Mohwasa, who gave me an opportunity to start a professional journey in his publishing house. I remain eternally grateful. Thank you to Mqondisi Dube who did not only refine my talent but also groomed me. Thanks to Monnakgotla Mojaki for being a big brother since The Mirror days.I must profusely thank Lawrence Ookeditse who helped edit this book. Lawrence has always insisted that I was destined for the international stage as a writer and a football administrator. Gratitude goes to Kenneth Middleton who ingeniously designed this book.Thank you to my good friend Mogomotsi Seretse, an immense playmaker in this project. I do not have sufficient words with which to thank you. Thanks to my good big brother Dr Gabriel Malebang who has been an inspiration in both my media work and life in general. You have waited and waited for this book. The late Log Raditlhokwa was my major source of inspiration as a writer; so thank you to the Raditlhokwa family.Thanks to *Honorable* Botsalo Ntuane-who is not only inspiration as a fine writer, but has always believed in my all-round talent-that i was destined for the international market in football. Look at me now! Haha..Thanks to my very good friends Bobo Moswaane,Jacques Kelebeng,*abuti* Tau Mosimanetau,*abuti* Sam Morotsi,Shadreck Balisi,*abut*i Matthews Balisi,Oliver Modise, Onalekitso Mmetli,Kagiso Mmopiemang,Refilwe G Molefi, Mathiba Onneile, Ace Orapeleng, Jabu Pilane, Mogogi Gabonamong, Ogomoditse Obusitse, Kegaisitse Dikosha, *abuti* Kennedy Motang, Mthokozisi Dube, Witness Tobaka, *abuti* Oteng Motshewa, Victor Baatweng, Mbongeni Mguni,*Attorney* Busang Manewe, *Attorney* Friday Leburu, *Attorney* Jabu Oteng, *Attorney* Martin Dingake, Gaongalelwe Keorapetse, Kabelo Mooketsi, Mpho Seno, Maureen Bome, *Sis* Tumy Modise, Panado Modukanele, Daniel Kenosi, Dozer Mokaraga, Owe Mmolawa,Lincoln Diteko, my brother

Ziyaad Desai, *Sis* Shadi Linchwe, *Sis* Nnunu Ramogotsi, my cousins Segomotso Rakitla, Obakeng Sikwane and Agrinette Lalu Kgakole, *abuti* Kgosietsile Mariri, *abuti* Banks Ndebele, Kitso Nkagelang, Othusitse Onalenna, Tyro Lepotokisi, Dipsey Selolwane, *abuti* Diphetogo Maswabi, Thuso Palai, Bay Tsimane, Arafat Khan, Tumiso Rakgare, Chase Pelekekae, Luthando Zibeko, Fox Phatsimo, Otsile Modisaotsile, Seabelo Modibe, Tumo Mpatane, Julian Bailey, coach Dragojlo Stanojlovic & family, Setete Phuthego, Raymond Tsheko, Botlhale Koothupile, *abuti* Jimmy George, Duncan Kgangkenna, Keorapetse Setlhare, Oteng Chilume, coach Rudolph Zapata, Molefi Nkwete, Daruosh Ghodrati, Nchidzi Smarts, Tshepo Maubane, Aubrey Lute, Matlhogonolo Sebate and my special brothers Khalid Niyonzima and Stephen Maposa for your profound and unconditional support. To *malome* Seremane Sikwane and Sergen Sikwane, I thank you for the support. To my innovative cousin Lesedi Matlapeng, thank you for your support. Thank you to the affable and special sister, Kemiso Motaung of Kaizer Chiefs. Sis Kemiso was very helpful with initial options around this book idea before it took a different form. The persistence of DJ Sbu has also been invaluable. Your books and motivation have been nothing but compelling tools for me to follow my dream. Thank you grootman. Robert Marawa's supreme authority on the beautiful game has been quite persuasive. I have learnt a lot of things through the many interviews you have had with Doctor Khumalo and other stakeholders over the years. So, thank you. Carlos Amato's prolific writings have been a compelling source of inspiration. A great writer, thank you. Thanks to Bamuza Sono who has been a good friend in football and various business ventures; through these, I have been able to get closer to the game and the important people around it. Thanks to my *Attorney* Shimane Ramafala in Johannesburg for the motivation and wise counsel. *Attorney* Mlungisi Cele in Johannesburg, thank you for keeping me going when I was in danger of flagging. *Attorney* Ashley Dipela in Bloemfontein, thank you for the motivation throughout the years while I was writing this book. Thank you to long-time friend Tuelo Serufho-who has been an inspiration in sports for many years now. Thanks Sethunya Kobedi, your critical assessment of the first manuscript was priceless. Thanks to my brother Modiri Tshutlhedi, a good brother forever. You have quietly but fully appreciated and understood my dream. Thanks to Palesa

Mngomezulu with whom i often shared and discussed initial possibilities around this book. Thank you to my good friend Ntsiki Mokoena, a good motivator since University. Thanks to my long time friend since University days, Siphamandla Made, a profound thinker and a complete sportsman who has supported me from day one. Thank you to the beautiful and esteemed Zandi Naka-a great friend in literature from way back at University.Thank you Isaac Pheko,Thabo Osekeng, *abuti* Fundi Gaoforwe, *abuti* Peter Batshane, Leatile Mmutle, *abuti* Anthony Rasetshwane, *abuti* Sidney Magagane, Sabelo Mlonyeni, Aubrey Kekana and Nicolus Kgopotso for your palpable belief in my ability as a sports leader. To *abuti* Fobby Radipotsane, *Sis* Emang Bokhutlo,Tumi Kegakilwe, *sis* Basadi Masimolole,Ntibi Kedikilwe,*abuti* Kgosana Masaseng, Christopher Hubona, Andile Mautle, Pontsho Moloi, Clifford Mogomotsi(posthumously) and Bongani Malunga, thank you for the support over the years. Kenanao Phele & Keikantse Phele, you have been great sisters in literature, thank you. Thank you Dr Lebohang Letsie who is a massive Kaizer Chiefs supporter, also an insightful fountain of history. Thank you to Dr Pinkie Mekgwe who has also been supportive all round. I must thank Keatlaretse Nyambe and Kuda Pie whose understanding of South African football is almost Solomonic-i drew a lot from you. Thank you to these people I consider family in football; Errol Dicks & sons, Somerset Gobuiwang & daughters, MacLean Letshwiti & family and Rashid Chopdat Ismail; these have been a great inspiration in my football pursuits and adventures for many,many years now. My good friends Bayan Jamali and Payam Jamali, thank you for the durable support and belief in me. I must also thank *abuti* Njabulo Gilika and chairman Kelesitse Gilika for their support. Thank you to chairman Rapula Okaile, *abuti* Gideon Mmolawa, *abuti* City Senne, *sis* Nancy Borakanelo, *sis* Mpho Moatshe, Kato Masibi, Maureen Ntsimako and the entire Gaborone United family for giving me an immense opportunity to lead such an esteemed club. I must also thank Nicholas Zackhem whose football pursuits have been inspiring. I wish to thank from the deepest corner of my heart all my teachers over the years notably Ronald Tsheko and my former Law lecturers notably Professor Pierre De Vos and Professor Patricia Lenaghan respectively. I must thank some of the best writers whose writings have inspired me as a young writer amongst others; Michael

Dingake, Gideon Nkala, *Advocate* Duma Boko, David Magang,Mesh Moeti and Outsa Mokone. I must also thank the most prolific writer and thinker Tupac Shakur,posthumously. Tupac has not only inspired me as a writer over the years but his book(The Rose That Grew From Concrete) has also inspired the design and the shape of this book.Salute!Thank you to my publishers Authorhouse in Indianapolis,United States especially Michael Lindenmuth, Myra Baldwin and Karen Adamson who have been very patient,very kind and very professional from day one. Without reservation,i wish to thank everybody who has been helpful. Those whom I may not have mentioned here, you know whoever you are, wherever you are,that i would not have accomplished this timeless tribute without you and your support. Pula!!!!!!!!

INDEX

CONTACT THE AUTHOR

For bookings and presentations; kindly contact Olebile Sikwane on:

Twitter; @OlebileSikwane
Facebook; Olebile Sikwane
Email address; ntsodi@gmail.com

ABOUT THE AUTHOR

OLEBILE NTSODI SIKWANE was born in Botswana. He matriculated at the prestigious Rosebank House College in Cape Town before pursuing a Bachelor of Laws(LLB) degree at the University of the Western Cape. Whilst at University, Sikwane worked for 365 Digital as a Match Reporter. He subsequently contributed to amongst others; Soccer Laduma, Kickoff (both magazine & website), Soccer Solutions and GroundUp. Sikwane has also worked for FIFA match agency Simsport International as a Match Planner.He later worked as a Case Manager at Berlin Sports Consulting Africa (now FC Cape Town Consulting) with a specific focus on FIFA solidarity fees, training and compensation. He subsequently worked as a General Manager for Gaborone United SC in the Botswana Premier League. Sikwane is part of an emerging African literati and a young but promising breed of football executives. Known for his avant-garde thinking and sharp negotiation skills,Sikwane together with Mark Byrne re-introduced Umbro in Botswana in 2011. In 2016, he introduced another brand Canterbury in Botswana as an exclusive franchise holder. Sikwane writes an insightful weekly soccer column *Final Whistle* published by Botswana's biggest newspaper,The Sunday Standard. Sikwane is based in Cape Town as a Football Intermediary.

Printed in the United States
By Bookmasters